GENESIS

Genesis

A Beginner's Guide to the Beginning

978-1-7910-3236-4 *print*
978-1-7910-3238-8 *eBook*

Genesis DVD

978-1-7910-3240-1

Also by Amy-Jill Levine

Short Stories by Jesus: The Enigmatic Parables of a Controversial Rabbi

Entering the Passion of Jesus: A Beginner's Guide to Holy Week

Light of the World: A Beginner's Guide to Advent

Sermon on the Mount: A Beginner's Guide to the Kingdom of Heaven

The Difficult Words of Jesus: A Beginner's Guide to His Most Perplexing Teachings

Witness at the Cross: A Beginner's Guide to Holy Friday

Signs and Wonders: A Beginner's Guide to the Miracles of Jesus

The Gospel of Mark: A Beginner's Guide to the Good News

The Gospel of John: A Beginner's Guide to the Way, the Truth, and the Life

A Child Is Born: A Beginner's Guide to Nativity Stories

With Warren Carter
The New Testament: Methods and Meanings

With Marc Zvi Brettler
The Bible With and Without Jesus: How Jews and Christians Read the Same Stories Differently

AMY-JILL LEVINE

GENESIS

A BEGINNER'S GUIDE TO THE BEGINNING

ABINGDON PRESS | NASHVILLE

Genesis
A Beginner's Guide to the Beginning

Library of Congress Control Number: 2026942499
978-1-7910-3236-4

Continued on page vi.

For Rev. Dr. Tammy Gieselman
and Rev. Mitchell C. Gieselman

Continued from page iv.

Cover art: Charles Francis Annesley Voysey (English, 1857-1941), *Adam and Eve*, ca. 1923, watercolor on paper, private collection. The Stapleton Collection/ Bridgeman Images.

Cover description: Features an illustrated garden of Eden scene filled with plants, flowers, birds, and Adam and Eve near the bottom center. The title "Genesis" appears in large purple text, with the subtitle "A Beginner's Guide to the Beginning" in a purple bar and the author's name Amy-Jill Levine displayed above in white type within a purple circle.

MANUFACTURED IN THE UNITED STATES OF AMERICA

CONTENTS

WATCH YOUR STUDY ANYTIME, ANYWHERE.

Access your *Genesis* videos and leader resources on any device with your Amplify Media account.

Get Started In Two Steps

1 Scan the QR code or go to My.AmplifyMedia.com /amplify/redeem

2 Create your free account and enter your companion code

Companion Code
ALIMXU5F

Once You're In

- Videos and leader resources saved to your account
- Watch anytime on phone, tablet, or TV
- Come back anytime at My.AmplifyMedia.com

Keep Track of Your Log In Info

Email ______________________________

Password ______________________________

Companion code subject to expiration. Code may be redeemed only by the recipient of this book. Code may not be transferred or sold separately. Internet connection required.

AMPLIFY™ MEDIA

INTRODUCTION

The story of the Tower of Babel, Genesis 11:1-9, begins, "Now the whole earth had one language and the same words." Such unification did not mean that comprehension was perfect. Words can have multiple meanings. For example, "cleave" means both to stick together and to separate; words said in anger carry different connotations than words said in love. Lines said by one actor can sound completely different than the same lines on the lips of another. How we read and how we interpret what we read depend substantially on how we understand the terms involved.

These points about words extend to narratives. One of the glorious aspects of studying biblical stories is that mutually exclusive interpretations of the same text can both be right. Events in the garden of Eden could be the source of original sin; they could also be the source of "original opportunity." The Holy Spirit may be present in Genesis 1, or he (she, it?) may not be. If biblical texts had only one meaning, there'd be no need for sermons or homilies, let alone people like me who write books about the Bible. Moreover, if they only had one meaning, they would be boring.

This study looks at six stories in Genesis: the creation of humanity and the subsequent events in Eden; Cain and Abel; Noah, the flood, and its aftermath; Abraham's almost-sacrifice of his beloved son Isaac; Jacob's dream of a stairway (it's not a ladder) to heaven; and Mrs. Potiphar's sexual harassment of Joseph. It offers interpretations that concern history, literature, and theology, and it invites you to share your own interpretations as well. If you begin with the question, "What does this text mean to me?" you've already got a start on interpretation. Then you can put your interpretation into conversation with those offered in this book and those offered by others, whether throughout the centuries or in your own reading circles.

One of my goals is to share with you how spectacular the Hebrew text of Genesis is. I've read Genesis in both Hebrew and English well over seventy times for class preparation, and I've looked at the Greek translation as well as various modern translations almost as often. I've taught Genesis in undergraduate and graduate seminars, in churches and synagogues; I've listened to it chanted, and then heard commentary on it, in synagogues. In Orthodox and Conservative synagogues, the entire Pentateuch is chanted in Hebrew every year; Reform congregations read on a triennial cycle (comparable to years A, B, and C for churches that use a lectionary). The text never gets old, which sounds weird for a text that is very, very old.

In preparing this volume, I found new connections among words and motifs. I also found myself increasingly sympathetic to the "villains," from the woman and the snake in Eden to Cain, the first fratricide, and Mrs. Potiphar, who epitomizes sexual harassment. I found myself arguing with Abraham about his willingness to sacrifice his son and with Jacob over his various shenanigans. I also found myself conversing with God, from the affirmative "love the creation, with everything very good" to the questions: Why put temptation in the garden? Why not accept Cain's offering? Why flood the world? Why command Abraham to sacrifice his son? Why make Jacob's life so difficult? Where were you when Joseph's brothers wanted to kill him, when he is falsely accused of rape, and when he is sent to prison? The answers I gained were complex and profound, and they made me want to ask more and more.

In the experience of reading and then rereading, we realize both that the meanings of texts are not static and that all readings are limited. We will never learn everything there is to know about these ancient stories, but something about them compels us to return, and to interpret anew, time after time.

Asking questions of a text—about character and plot, motive and intonation, other texts that provide insight—should be part of the reading process. When the text is the Bible, then such engagement is actually a form of worship. If we then talk with others about our interpretations, we are building community, and this, too, is all to the good.

To continue the conversation, I have dedicated the introduction of this book to the story of the Tower of Babel in Genesis 11; the book's conclusion offers suggestions for how the stories it addresses can find complementary readings in other biblical passages. If these suggestions encourage you to read, or reread, other stories, so much the better.

The Tower of Babel

I am a language nerd: I like word origins (and I am careful to distinguish between etymology and entomology), and I appreciate how words take on various connotations in literary contexts. Each time I translate a text, whether Genesis from its original Hebrew or its Greek translation (the Septuagint, the text used by most of the authors of New Testament texts) or Mark's Gospel from its original Greek, my translations change. Insights from new scholarly publications, comments made in the classroom or in Bible study groups, and advances in linguistics all influence the translations. In the following pages, I'll bring out the nuances of the Hebrew of Genesis and explain where I disagree with the New Revised Standard Version Updated Edition, the most recent translation and the one most often used in university classrooms. You may well disagree with me, which is fine. Translation is an art, not a science.

When we step into a text, one approach is to assess the setting first. For example, Genesis 11:1 states that the "whole earth" had "one language and the same words." My first thought is one of paradise. Genesis 11 could be a chapter describing a new garden of Eden where translation apps (or the Star Trek Universal Translator) are unnecessary and where there are no foreign language requirements in any academic program. On the other hand, we can read the introduction as a polemic against systems that encourage, or force, their populations to speak *only* their language.

Personally, I prefer that we have different languages. In graduate school, my husband courted me by whispering in my ear, with a French accent, the names of French critical theorists: Lacan, Foucault, Derrida. The language was seductive. I suspect if he whispered the names of German philosophers—Kant, Hegel, Schleiermacher—the courtship would not have been nearly as romantic.

We next learn that people "migrated from the east" and "came upon a plain in the land of Shinar and settled there" (11:2). The theme of migration, and in particular of people coming from the East, wanders through the Bible. Eden is "in the east" (2:8), and Cain is exiled "east of Eden" (3:24; this is the source for the title of John Steinbeck's 1952 novel and the [great] 1955 movie with James Dean). Noah's ark lands somewhere on the mountains of Ararat (not "Mount Ararat" and so a problem for ark-hunters and TV specials about them). Abraham migrates west from Ur of the Chaldees to Canaan, then south to Egypt, and then back to Canaan. Jacob, who, with his mother's conniving, tricks his father, Isaac, into giving him the blessing that should have gone to his brother, the firstborn twin, Esau, flees his home in Haran to his Uncle Laban's house in Paddan-Aram, returns to Canaan, and will die in Egypt. Joseph's brothers traffic him; enslavers take him to Egypt. He relocates his entire family to Egypt, and when his father Jacob dies,

Joseph and his brothers return his body to Canaan for his burial. The penultimate line in Genesis is Joseph's command to the Israelite population, "When God comes to you, you shall carry up my bones from here" (Genesis 50:25), so that he, too, will be buried in Canaan. The Bible is a book about wandering, of finding, or, better, making a home. It also tells us that once we are settled, we might just want to keep a travel bag packed. We may stay in one place, but our children may move. And it tells us that wherever we are, east of Eden, in Egypt, in the Promised Land, God is with us.

The land of Shinar is Babylon (see 10:10, which mentions Babel); on the map, today it is Iraq. In the early sixth century BCE, the Babylonians conquered the kingdom of Judah, burned down the Temple of Solomon in the capital, Jerusalem, and forced a substantial part of the population into exile. Yet it is likely in Babylon that scribes put together most of the Torah, the first five books of the Bible (what Jews call the Tanakh and what Christians call the Old Testament). The notice of Babylon here, early in Genesis, is one of several early indications that the Bible was not written in a cultural vacuum. As we'll see, Genesis 1:1, which opens with a temporal clause "When God began to create..." offers an alternative to the Babylonian creation epic, the *Enumah Elish*, which means "When on High" and goes on to speak of the founding of the city of Babylon. The Hebrews sacralized time, which is a smart move for a people in exile, since time is everywhere. The Babylonians sacralized space, which is a smart move for people promoting an empire.

Bible readers know that Shinar suggests Babylon, the place of exile. The more we know of the later stories, the more interesting these earlier references become. Do we want to make our home here, or do we want to return? Do we want to promote the will of the conqueror, or do we recognize it as problematic?

The people "said to one another, 'Come, let us make bricks and fire them thoroughly'" so that they "had brick for stone and bitumen for mortar" (11:3). The Hebrew is literally "let us brick bricks" (the fun of language: a noun with an accompanying verb). The quantity of bricks needed for the architectural project of building "a city and a tower with its top in the heavens..." (11:4) is staggering. And I'm also concerned, since references to brick and mortar will show up again in the beginning of Exodus, when the Egyptians forced the Israelites they enslaved to make bricks to build storehouse cities. Exodus 1:14 explains that the Egyptians made the lives of the Israelites "bitter with hard servitude in mortar and bricks and in every kind of field labor. They were ruthless in all the tasks that they imposed on them." Knowing what we know about Exodus, I'm not optimistic about this tower in Shinar.

Connections between Genesis and Exodus continue. The other time the Hebrew text uses the word "bitumen" is to describe how Moses's mother constructed an "ark" (yes, same word as in the Noah story!) out of bitumen and then placed the baby in this ark (Exodus 2:3). She is doing her best to thwart the decree made by Pharaoh, the Egyptian ruler, that all Hebrew baby boys be drowned (see Exodus 1:22). When we read the Bible all the way through and return to read again, our comprehension necessarily increases. We're only in Genesis 11, and we can reflect on building projects: Enormous towers for whom? For what purpose? At what cost? With what labor force?

The people in Shinar wanted to build this giant tower, not because of a lack of office space or affordable housing. They wanted to "make a name for ourselves; otherwise, we shall be scattered abroad upon the face of the earth" (11:4). The initial irony is fabulous, since in this story, unlike the chapter that precedes it, with its recording of name after name in the "Table of Nations" (e.g., Genesis 10:2, "The descendants of Japheth: Gomer, Magog, Madai, Javan, Tubal, Meshech, and Tiras"), the builders of the Tower of Babel are never named.

We also know that their plan is contrary to divine will. When we dip back into Genesis, we see the folly of the plan to avoid being "scattered" (the Greek translation for "scattered" is the verbal form of the term "diaspora"). In Genesis 1:28, God blesses human beings and commissions them, "Be fruitful and multiply and fill the earth." They cannot fulfill this commission if they remain in Shinar. More, if they continue to reproduce but stay put, overcrowding will make life impossible.

The story can function as a satire of the pretensions of the Babylonian Empire and, by extension, all empires that want to rule the world and all earthly kings who think they are divine. The giant tower would remind the people of ancient Israel of the Babylonian towers known as ziggurats (I'm waiting for a *New Yorker* cartoon depicting the Tower of Babel on fire and the caption, "Ziggurats are dangerous to your health"). Such satirizing of Babylon's imperial goals continues in the Prophetic literature. Isaiah writes,

> *How you are fallen from heaven,*
> *O Morning Star, son of Dawn!*
> *How you are cut down to the ground,*
> *you who laid the nations low!*
> *You said to yourself,*
> *'I will ascend to heaven;*
> *I will raise my throne above the stars of God. . . .*
> *I will ascend to the tops of the clouds;*
> *I will make myself like the Most High.'*
> *But you are brought down to the Sheol,*
> *to the depths of the Pit.*
> *Those who see you will stare at you*
> *and ponder over you: '*
> *Is this the man who made the earth tremble. . . .'*
> *(Isaiah 14:12-16)*

While reception history reads this passage as speaking about the fall of Satan ("morning star" via the Latin gets us "Lucifer"), Isaiah had contemporary politicians in mind. Similarly, Jeremiah, who witnessed the siege of Jerusalem, writes, "Though Babylon should mount up to heaven, / and though she should fortify her strong height, / from me destroyers would come upon her, / says the LORD" (Jeremiah 51:53). The more we know of the Bible's literary and historical contexts, the more interesting, and profound, it becomes.

Back to Genesis 11. God is not thrilled with humanity's plan to build a tower to the heavens and so encroach on heavenly space. "The LORD came down to see the…tower…"—a great line; the people are building and building, but God still has to "come down"—and then explains to the heavenly council, who have been part of the story since creation (see the next chapter): "Look, they are one people, and they have all one language, and this is only the beginning of what they will do; nothing that they propose to do will now be impossible for them" (11:6). I like this verse. I like the idea that we can, to use the modern idiom, shoot for the stars. We humans have talent and drive and ingenuity.

And yet, when we think of ourselves as gods, when we get out of our lane and think we are equal to God, we risk becoming deadly. Genesis 1 states that we are created in the image and likeness of the divine and that we are to have mastery over the earth and all of God's other creations. Given these benefits and this charge, it's difficult enough to be the best humans we can be. I'm happy to leave matters of final judgment, or ultimate justice, or ultimate mercy, to God. I'm happy to see what good we can bring about on earth.

God's response to humanity's hubris is to "confuse their language there, so that they will not understand one another's speech" (11:7). Genesis 10:5 already mentioned these multiple languages, for example, "These are the descendants of Japheth in their lands, with their own language, by their families, in their nations." The idea of what today we might call "multiculturalism" is part of the fabric of creation.

While the response to the tower was to confound communication, the irony continues, since we can understand each other. We have been discussing, and will continue to discuss, the English translation of an originally Hebrew text. Some of us have phones or watches that do immediate translation. The writers of the Bible, ancient Israel's literate classes, knew not only their native language; they also knew the languages of the nearby peoples.

There may be more irony yet. The term the NRSVue renders "understand," which is a logical translation for "they will not understand one another's speech," is the Hebrew *shema*, "to hear." It is the beginning of the famous call, "Hear, O Israel, the Lord is our God, the Lord alone" (or the "Lord is one" [Deuteronomy 6:4]). The term *shema* will reappear throughout the Bible. It starts in Eden, when the first couple hear the sound of God walking in the garden (3:8). Because the man heard, or listened to, the woman, he moves from infancy to maturity, with both the gains and the losses this entails (3:17). In Genesis 42:21, Joseph's brothers lament that they did not listen (*shema*) to Joseph when he pleaded with them not to harm him. Ishmael, the name of the son born to Abraham and Hagar, means "God hears" (16:11). When we work through the text slowly and listen closely—I know, difficult in this age of one-liners and AI summaries—we can savor the Bible's words. Hearing and listening carefully bring us to understanding. Such intentional listening should also make us more attentive to what we say and how what we say may be heard by others.

The story ends with the notice that the location was called "Babel" because there God confused human language and scattered the people "over the face of all the earth" (11:9). A cognate term in Hebrew means "confused" or "mixed up." Today we speak of "babbling." While there is no clear connection between this term and our Tower of Babel, "Babel" and "babbling" may both be onomatopoeic (love that word)—that is, words that sound like what they are. For example, the Hebrew word for "fly" is *zvuv*, which sounds like the noise a fly makes (English speakers may use "buzz"). "Babel" sounds like the vocalizations people make to infants (along the lines of "googoo" or "gaga"). The name "babel" also sounds like "Babylon."

Another irony: The first instruction humans receive is "be fruitful and multiply and fill the earth" (1:28). Scattering can be a punishment, or the result of war, but it can also be the promise of new life and a way of spreading blessing. Scattering takes us out of "group think" (the hive mind, the Borg from *Star Trek*, the TV show *Pluribus*) where everyone works on the same project—"to make a name for ourselves." This type of unity denies the individual names of the people who did the work. Scattering may allow us to be our fully creative selves.

The people of Shinar wanted to make a name for themselves. We can identify no single individual there. The next chapter of Genesis introduces Abraham, to whom God promises, "I will make of you a great nation, and I will bless you and make your name great, so that you will be a blessing" (12:2). A name for a blessing sounds to me like a better legacy than a tower reaching upward but never being high enough. The people in Genesis 11 wanted to build a tower to the heavens, but it is God who creates, and controls, the stairway between heaven and earth.

In the Beginning

These brief observations about the Tower of Babel set us off in multiple directions: We return to the beginning to read closely Genesis 1, and there we find humanity's potential and responsibility. In Genesis 2, we see divine care, with the notice that "it is not good that the man should be alone." Genesis 3—snake, fruit, nudity, shame—takes us from infancy to maturity, into wisdom and responsibility, out of Eden and into the world.

The story of Cain and Abel, the subject of Genesis 4 and our chapter 2, opens questions of jealousy and rivalry, of mortality and stability, of punishment and justice. Chapter 3 brings us to Noah. Cain asked if he was his brother's keeper; I'm wondering if Noah ever asked the same question as he watched his neighbors drown. His story concerns how the attempt to be like the gods, an issue in the garden of Eden and repeated in Genesis 11, can lead to moral decline, and how good things (wine that brings comfort) can become harmful (wine leading to drunkenness, leading to cursing, and so on). It also poses to us the uncomfortable and all too real question: in the face of human evil, is mass destruction ever warranted?

Among the various stories concerning Abraham, our journey through Genesis lingers on Mount Moriah, where Abraham responds to God's command to sacrifice his son Isaac. Known as the *Akedah* (Hebrew for "binding"), Genesis 22 raises questions about the righteousness both of God and of Abraham, of how we may sacrifice our children, of when to resist and when to submit. Whether Abraham "passed" the test is a question you may want to consider.

Next, we come to the famous scene known as "Jacob's Ladder." It's not a ladder. The mental image of angels negotiating the ups and downs on the rungs shows why "ladder" is the wrong translation. Jacob dreams of a staircase, and that dream opens to a discussion of sacred space, of divine/human communication, and of divine grace, given Jacob's not entirely honest actions.

Our sixth chapter takes us to Joseph. Here we meet Mrs. Potiphar, who attempts to seduce Joseph and, when he refuses her advances, grabs his garment and uses it as evidence that he had attempted to rape her. The story pulls together numerous threads (this is a great pun, by the way) of the other stories, from the nudity and then being clothed of Adam and Eve, to Cain's bodily mark of protection, to the temptations and testing at the *Akedah*, to how Jacob uses clothing to trick his father and how Jacob's sons trick him with Joseph's coat.

The people we meet along the way are not perfect, by any means. They lie and they blame others for their actions; they deceive and betray; they murder and engage in human trafficking. They do not always listen. They are human beings, at their best and their worst. They are endlessly frustrating and endlessly fascinating. They are invitations to discussion. In their stories, we may be reminded of people we have known; we may be reminded of ourselves.

CHAPTER 1

Adam and Eve

Genesis offers two creation stories. The first, Genesis 1:1–2:4a, is an orderly account describing the creation of the world in six days. On day six, God creates the animals, and then, in consultation with the heavenly court, God creates human beings, male and female. On day seven, God rests and establishes the Sabbath as sacred time. The text is repetitive and so easy to memorize. It also makes a dandy bedtime story: Little children can easily remember the end of each day, "And God saw that it was good" (1:10, 12, 18, 21, 25) and then can delight with the variation on the theme: day six, the day God created human beings, concludes, "God saw everything that he had made, and indeed, it was very good" (1:31). At the end, God blesses the seventh day, "because on it God rested from all the work that he had done in creation" (2:3). We can add, "and now, little one, time to rest from all the work you have done today." (Trust me, this works.)

In comparison, Genesis 2:4b–3:24 is a narrative featuring characterization and conflict. It starts off well with God creating the earthling (*ha'adam*) from the earth (*'adamah*) and then planting a garden in Eden. Other translations that better catch the pun include "human" from "humas" (not "hummus").

God places the earthling in the garden to "till it and keep it." Eden is not a place without work; it is a place where work is easy. Following the notice that the human being can eat fruit from every tree in the garden except from the "tree of the knowledge of good and evil" (2:17),

God creates a woman to be the human being's companion. So far, so good. In Genesis 3, the snake logically points out to the woman that eating the fruit (it is identified as an apple in the twelfth century) would be beneficial. She eats, and she gives some to the man who eats as well. God is not pleased. The end of the chapter sees God expelling the man and woman from Eden, and so human history begins.

There is too much in this story to discuss in one volume, let alone one chapter, so we'll focus on how Genesis 1–3 prompts questions about humanity: Who are we? What is our purpose? How do we relate to each other and to God? We'll also explore how the creation narrative sets up the struggles that human beings continue to have and so how it anticipates concerns that surface in the stories of Cain and Abel, Noah, the near-sacrifice of Isaac, Jacob's dream of a stairway to heaven, the story of Joseph and Mrs. Potiphar, and, as we've already encountered, the Tower of Babel.

The Image and Likeness of God

Students of the Bible, myself included, often like to talk about the sources behind the text. We typically suggest that the first creation story was written by a priestly writer (designed P, for "priestly") during or immediately after the Babylonian exile (586–538 BCE), to provide the community a vision of universal organization amid the chaos of displacement, a sense of sacred life apart from the Promised Land and without the Temple, and a version of their own history to provide a religious and cultural anchor. A giant tower cannot make a people endure, but stories can.

The Bible's opening story tells us that everything is divinely created, and everything is good: sea and air, plants and animals. This beginning should be a prompt for us to take care of God's creation. Generally, if we want to show appreciation for the good gifts we are given (especially if we love the one who gave us those gifts), we take care of what we are given. But now I'm preaching—moving on.

Following an orderly creation carried out by a process of separation—water from dry land, heaven from earth, day from night—on the sixth day, God creates the "living creatures of every kind: cattle and creeping things and wild animals of the earth of every kind" (1:25). Then, as the epitome of creation, comes humanity.

In Genesis 1:26, God says, "Let us make humans [*'adam*] in our image, according to our likeness, and let them have dominion over the fish of the sea and over the birds of the air and over the cattle and over all the wild animals of the earth and over every creeping thing that creeps upon the earth." Christians traditionally see the "us" as indicating the Trinity; Jews have multiple alternative explanations. How we interpret the Bible usually depends on the lenses through which we read it. Both readings are right, given the theological concerns of the readers. Reading retrospectively (using later material to interpret earlier material) is legitimate; it is one way of reading out of many.

Ancient audiences would have understood God as speaking to the heavenly court. People in antiquity, and many to this day, imagined God as a great king, and kings had attendants.

The reason many of us today do not think about this court is that translations sometimes mislead us. In the synagogue, the congregation chants Exodus 15:11ff; in Jewish settings, the passage is called the *Mi Chamocha*, from its first words, Who (*mi*) is like you (*cha-mocha*; the "ch" is has a guttural sound, as in the name [Johannes Sebastian] Bach). The translation I remember from my childhood read, "Who is like you, O Lord, *among the mighty*? Who is like you, majestic in holiness, awesome in splendor, doing wonders?" I did not know who the "mighty" were. When I was very young, I watched Mighty Mouse, and

I knew he "came to save the day," so I figured that God had helpers like Mighty Mouse. (Not a bad conclusion for a child.) The greater problem is that the Hebrew does not say "among the mighty." It says, "among the gods" (Hebrew: *b'elim*). Similarly, Psalm 29:1 in the NRSVue speaks of "heavenly beings"; the Hebrew is *b'nei elim*, "children of God." For another slippery translation, Job 1:6 reports that "the heavenly beings" (NRSVue; the Hebrew is *b'nai ha-elohim*, literally "sons of God") presented themselves to God.

That same heavenly council to whom God speaks in Genesis 1 reappears in the "us" of Genesis 3:22, where God states, "the humans have become like one of us." In Genesis 11:7, the Tower of Babel story, God says, "Let us go down and confuse their language." For one more example, 1 Kings 22:19 quotes the prophet Micaiah, "I saw the LORD sitting on his throne, with all the host of heaven standing beside him . . ." Ancient Israelites believed in multiple divine beings, but only one was to receive worship. People who today believe in angels and demons should be comfortable with the idea of this heavenly council.

Genesis 1:27 reports that God created "humans (Hebrew *'adam*, not a proper name yet) . . . male and female." God looks like us, and we look like God. Ezekiel 1:26 affirms that God appeared "like a human form." When divine messengers, later known as "angels," appear, they look like people—gorgeous (see Judges 13; see also Genesis 18:2)—but people nonetheless. No wings or haloes. The ethical takeaway is that we need to see that divine image in everyone, including people we despise or who despise us. When we hate, we lose part of that divine image. The concept is exemplified by Cain, whose image changes when God rejects his sacrifice (4:5, "his countenance fell").

Later commentators insist that to be in the divine image means we should act like God. For example, as God is compassionate, so we should be compassionate. On the other hand, God can be vengeful, as in Deuteronomy 32:35 (cf. Romans 12:19). However, while we are to show compassion, vengeance is not our job. In these verses from Deuteronomy and Romans, God claims vengeance. Compassion without accountability is just as problematic as accountability without compassion. God has the task of final judgment, and that's well above my pay grade.

I Will Make a Helper

In Genesis 2, God creates a singular human (*'adam*), then the animals, then from the human's body God creates a woman. We can view the woman in Genesis 2 as the final version after the man's first draft; we can view her as a secondary creation. I'd prefer to follow the egalitarian model of Genesis 1, in which both male and female are in the divine image and the two are seen as equal.

According to Genesis 2:7, the Lord God formed man (Hebrew *ha'adam*, "the adam" or "the human") from the dust (Hebrew *'adamah*, arable soil, topsoil, or earth) and breathed into its nostrils the breath of life, and the man (*'adam*) became a living being (*nefesh hayyah*). Humans and earth are interdependent. We care for the earth, and the earth provides for us. Along with humanity and earth, the partnership also includes God, and Genesis depicts a very hands-on God: fashioning the creature from the dirt, shaping a nose, and breathing into it. Thus, we have a different theology from Genesis 1, where God creates by word (e.g., "Be light" [1:3]). I like the idea of God as a potter (so did Isaiah, see Isaiah 64:8; Jeremiah 18; Sirach 33:13; Romans 9:21) and so as an artist. I also like the teaching that God is intimately involved with the fashioning of us, so that we can all say "I praise you, for I am fearfully and wonderfully made" (Psalm 139:14).

This *nephesh* of which we are constituted is not the "soul" as we come to think of it, an immortal something that survives the body. The term *nephesh* suggests animation, breathing in and out. The term had already appeared in Genesis 1:20-21 to describe the "living creatures": fish and birds and sea monsters. It describes the living creatures with whom God covenants following the flood (9:12). Deuteronomy 6:5 instructs, "You shall love the LORD your God with all your heart and with all your soul (*nephesh*) and with all your might." Rather than an abstract soul, we might think of this *nephesh*-based love as something included "with every breath we take," with everything that animates us. When we read Genesis 2, we might need to be reminded to slow down, to take account of our breathing, to "catch our breath" and think of what an amazing thing, and amazing gift, life is.

Following some agricultural and geographical details about creation, the narrator returns to our earthling whom God places in the "garden of Eden to till it and keep it" (2:15). The name Eden comes from a Hebrew root meaning "pleasure" or "delight" (the name "Edna" is a cognate). Psalm 36:8 praises God in sensual terms: "you give them drink from the river of your delights" (*'adanecha*, based on the same root as "Eden"). An even more physical connotation appears in Genesis 18:12. The matriarch Sarah, overhearing that her nonagenarian husband Abraham and she are about to become parents, laughs and thinks to herself, "After I have grown old, and my husband is old, shall I be fruitful?" The translators are modest. The Hebrew says, "After I have grown old, and my husband is old, shall I have pleasure (*'ednah*)?" (I remember the verse, Genesis 18:12, because of Tchaikovsky's 1812 Overture, with the canons booming, so the earth moves.)

In Eden, work is hard but rewarding. The term translated "till" is in Hebrew *eved*, a term that appears over one thousand times; it connotes not so much technical gardening (clearing, fertilizing, planting, weeding) but "serving"; its noun form gives us both "servant" and "slave" as well as "worker" and, amazingly, the Hebrew term for "worship." I like the idea of "serving" as well as "pre-serving" (preserving) the land: it produces food for us, and we serve it by providing it with water and nutrients and by protecting it. We might also think of reserving, setting aside space for animals and plants. Our relationship to "serving" the land can be extended to matters of "deserving" care.

Such linguistic playfulness is not merely a word game; it is something biblical Hebrew prompts. The connection between the land and the connotations of "work," "service," and "worship" shared by the same Hebrew root is supported by the Hebrew term in 2:15 for "keep," *shamar*, which conveys "guard" or "protect." Thus, Exodus 23:11 cautions against overfarming even as it acknowledges that the land contributes to human and animal flourishing: "the seventh year you shall let [the land] rest and lie fallow so that the poor of your people may eat, and what they leave the wild animals may eat. You shall do the same with your vineyard and with your olive orchard." The practice gives us the term "sabbatical."

Some people love to garden: to mulch and weed, to plant and water, to trim and prune. Some people like to get their hands into the soil, turn it over, and nurture newly planted seeds. I don't like gardening, I don't like bugs (back to entomology), and my one philodendron is not looking good. For those who like gardening, you have another way of returning to Eden. Those of us less inclined can nevertheless appreciate your creations.

God then gives the earthling, the "living being," dietary instructions: all fruit is fine, save for that of the tree of the knowledge of good and evil. Eat that, says God, and "you shall die." The Hebrew infinitive absolute is an intensive "Dying you will die" or, colloquially, "You'll drop dead" (2:17). It may also mean "you will become mortal." It is possible that humans were initially immortal, and what they lost in Eden was immortality. According to Genesis 5:5, Adam lived for 930 years, so the idea of immediate dying is relative.

Genesis 2:16 reads, "And the Lord God commanded the man, 'You may freely eat of every tree of the garden...'" I prefer to translate this opening as "God instructed" rather than "commanded." The Hebrew is the verb *tzavah*, the same root as the term *mitzvah*, as in *bar mitzvah* or *bat mitzvah*, the age at which Jewish boys and girls take on adult responsibilities. The NRSVue frequently translates the same verb as "instructed"; for example, Genesis 47:11, toward the conclusion of the Joseph story, reads, "Joseph settled his father and his brothers and granted them a holding in the land of Egypt, in the best part of the land...as Pharaoh had instructed (*tzavah*)." The idea of "instruction" suggests to me "good advice" or "If you do this, then such-and-such will happen"; it has a more pastoral and parental connotation than "command." I also find, when working with church groups, that "commandment" suggests to them "the Ten Commandments" and by extension "Jewish Law." On the heels of this association comes the unfortunate and incorrect stereotype of "Old Testament Law" versus "New Testament grace." The translation "instruction" provides a corrective. Instruction and grace are mutually informing, not mutually exclusive. That the man and woman do not, upon eating the forbidden fruit, immediately die, that Cain's life is preserved, etc., show that grace is built into the structure of creation. By the way, the term "Ten Commandments" never appears in the Bible, despite most English translations. The Hebrew is simply "ten words" or, from the Greek, *decalogue*.

At this point, the human being is a vegan. A few friends of my friends, also vegans, love to point this out. I point out that we're only in chapter 2. In chapter 9, following the flood, God tells Noah that meat is now on the table, as long as blood is avoided.

Now comes the first notice that something is "not good": God states, "It is not good that the man should be alone; I will make him a helper as his partner" (2:18). The partner is the *'adam*'s equal, someone who can mirror humanity back. "Helper" (Hebrew *'ezer*, as in the names "Ezra" and "Ebenezer") does not mean a subordinate. Psalm 121:2 identifies God as a "partner" (*'ezer*), "My help (*'ezer*) comes from the LORD, / who made heaven and earth." This is the psalm that begins, in most translations, "I lift up my eyes to the hills— / from where will my help come?" The NRSVue correctly adds the question mark (ancient Hebrew not only lacks punctuation; it also lacks vowels). To think that salvation will come from the hills, like the cavalry charging to the rescue, is to miscue the text. Salvation doesn't come from the hills; it comes from God.

God then experiments. That's what artists do. "So out of the ground the LORD God formed every animal of the field and every bird of the air and brought them to the man to see what he would call them, and whatever the man called every living creature, that was its name" (2:19). The animals are also living creatures, each a *nefesh hayyah*, each also created from the earth. God created the living creatures, but the human being names them. God and humanity work in harmonious partnership: God starts the process of creation, and the human being helps in bringing order to it. The human names all the living creatures (it's a fascinating exercise: find a picture of an animal, perhaps an unfamiliar one, and try to think of an apt name; I see where we get "sloth" and "hippopotamus [Greek: "river horse"], but "pink fairy armadillo"?). We might stop to recount how we came to name our children or our pets. This naming is part of the act of creation and of bringing order out of chaos.

After all that work of creating other living beings, it turns out that "for the man (*ha-'adam*) there was not found a helper as his partner" (2:19-20). I picture the animals parading before their fellow clay-creature and giving rise to speculation: the sheep might keep me warm, but she'd be a terrible conversationalist ("Baa" said the sheep); the dog could play fetch, but that going outside to poop can get annoying as can the shedding ("Woof," said the dog); the myna bird can talk, but its vocabulary is a tad repetitive ("Repetitive," said the bird). You can fill in the rest.

Some readers insist that what the human being wants is not companionship but reproductive capacity. Only a woman, and not a sheep, dog, or bird, is going to produce the next generation. Nor can the human being fulfill the command to be fruitful and multiply unless there's a complementary human to facilitate the process. However, the problem, the "not good" order of the universe that new creation will resolve is not reproduction. It is loneliness. After the Covid lockdowns, many of us have come to a greater recognition of the problem of "loneliness." God recognizes it too.

The primary purpose of this "helper" is thus not to make babies. That idea reduces women to wombs, and it eliminates any purpose for women who are either infertile or menopausal. We are created as social beings; we do better in community settings; we do better when we have the opportunity to love one another.

Because the human being found no "helper," God now resorts to surgery. No more creation from the topsoil; this time, God causes the human being to fall asleep, takes "one of his ribs (Hebrew: *tzela*) and closed up its place with flesh" (2:21), makes a woman out of this *tzela*, and presents her to the now-awake human being. Most English translations render *tzela* as "rib." The Hebrew term more precisely means "side" in the sense of an architectural feature that stands perpendicular to or opposite to another structure. Exodus 25–28, 36–38 uses the term often for Temple construction, as does Ezekiel 41. Nothing in any of these other sixty or so uses suggests a "rib."

The translation "side" gives us the model of the first two creatures walking side by side. Some later Jewish interpretations, influenced by

Plato's *Symposium*, suggest that humanity was originally created as pairs back-to-back. God splits the two down the middle so that we are always looking for our "other" (not "better") half. In some cases, the pairs were both women, others both men, and still others men and women. This reading both fits the concern that "it is not good for the human to be alone" and answers the question of what the woman does to "help" that the sheep, dog, or bird cannot do. The newly created human being is a partner who completes the original human's identity; in modern terms, the *ezer k'nego*, the "partner like him (or her) self" who encourages us when we need encouraging and offers alternatives when choices need to be made, and who resolves the problem of loneliness. The new creation mirrors back to the *'adam*, what being human means.

The human being, following the surgery, wakes up, and speaks: "This at last is bone of my bones / and flesh of my flesh; / this one shall be called Woman, / for out of Man this one was taken" (2:23). "Bone of my bone" might not be as romantic as "Derrida, Foucault..." but it's not bad. I'm not thrilled that he refers to the woman as "this," but he's likely befuddled over what has happened. The Hebrew word for "man" is *ish* and for "woman" *ishah*. The terms are not really cognates; neither are the English "man" and "woman": "man" was, in Old English, *wer* (as in werewolf) and woman was *wif* (as in midwife, which says nothing about marriage). But whether in modern English or in Hebrew, the sound-alike makes for a nice connection. Here in Eden, the man recognizes the woman as an equal: same bone, same flesh. More interesting than the sheep.

Genesis 2:24 provides an etiology: because of this creation of flesh from flesh and bone from bone, "a man leaves his father and his mother and clings to his wife, and they become one flesh." The verse is anachronistic, since there are yet no "parents" to leave, let alone in-laws to meet. It is also not the way things were usually done, since in most biblical stories, the woman leaves her parents and joins the family of her husband-to-be: Rebekah leaves her home to be with Isaac, Rachel and Leah leave their father Laban to be with Jacob. A matrilocal model would be particularly awkward in polygynous settings. According to 1 Kings 11:3, King Solomon had "seven hundred princesses" that were "among his wives": with a matrilocal system, I shudder to think of the mileage required.

The idea of "cleaving" (KJV; one of those marvelous contranyms with two opposite meanings, like "dust," "bolt," "buckle," and "peruse") suggests not so much physical union but rather the establishment of a new family. The couple is defined primarily by each other rather than by paternity or maternity. This definition is also the sign of maturity: they are no longer under their parents' roofs. The only way they can fulfill this idea of leaving parents and cleaving to each other is by leaving one home and making another. The story thus anticipates the exodus from Eden.

Naked and Not Ashamed

The chapter ends with the note that "the man (*'adam*) and his wife (*ishah*, "woman") were both naked and were not ashamed" (2:25). Other interpretations offer "they were not embarrassed" and even "they were not disappointed." That last one makes me smile.

The language "his wife" or "his woman" shows that the text is patriarchal; we could equally talk about the "woman and her husband." The term "wife" also introduces the idea of marriage. Already at the beginning of creation, we can speculate on what constitutes a marriage. Legality? Love? Companionship? Perhaps we might think of marriage, or a relationship in which one person can stand naked and not ashamed in front of another, as one resolution to the problem of loneliness.

When in the next chapter of Genesis, the man and woman eat the forbidden fruit, the first thing they realize is that they are naked. Their newly gained "knowledge of good and evil" is not the knowing of right from wrong per se. If it were, then the woman and man could not be blamed for eating the forbidden fruit. It is rather the knowledge that comes with maturity and so the loss of childhood innocence.

Infants are not ashamed of being naked, let alone having their diapers changed or being bathed. But around toddler time, which is also toilet-training time, they pick up from adults the knowledge that they are not to be naked in front of strangers, that they are not to pee and poop wherever and whenever they want, and that their bodies are precious and to be protected. The result of such lessons should be what we might call modesty; they should not be about shame. There is nothing wrong with the human body (again, it is in the image of the divine), but not everything needs to be displayed to the public.

When the term "naked" appears in the Bible, it usually concerns the nakedness of the poor and the captive. For example, Isaiah 58:7 reminds the people of their duty "to share your bread with the hungry / and bring the homeless poor into your house; / when you see the *naked*, to cover them. . . ." (emphasis added). To be naked is to be vulnerable and so in need of protection and support.

Genesis 1:26, the first creation narrative, assures us that we are in the divine image and likeness. Thus, we should be able to stand in front of a full-length mirror, naked, and say, "This is a divine image." It's a great way to start the day. The reference to being naked but not ashamed should also help us with matters of justice: when we see people in need, our role is to make them feel supported and not embarrassed. Finally, Genesis 2 tells us that when we can be naked before another, the one who is "bone of our bones and flesh of our flesh," and not be ashamed or embarrassed, we are back in Eden.

The Snake

Snakes are fascinating for various reasons: They shed their skin and so appear reborn; they are associated with the underworld; they can poison; and they are (at least to me) both viscerally frightening if encountered in the wild and endlessly watchable as long as they are safely at a distance or being held by someone else. In the Mesopotamian Gilgamesh epic, a snake steals the flower of immortality from Gilgamesh; in Greek thought, a snake wraps itself around a staff, the "rod of Aesclepius," and comes to symbolize medicine, as does the caduceus, a staff with two snakes. Today, "snake" has predominantly negative connotations: snake eyes, snake oil, snake pit. Yes, there's the helpful plumber's snake, but overall, the reputation is not great. I'd like to put in a good word or two for our snake in Eden.

Genesis 3 begins, "Now the serpent was more crafty than any other wild animal that the Lord God had made" (3:1a). That's a loaded verse. First, "serpent" is a synonym for "snake," but it sounds more creepy. The NRSVue translates the same term as "snake" for Exodus 4:3, where Moses throws his staff on the ground, "and it became a snake." Conversely, following a plague of poisonous snakes, on God's command, Moses makes "a serpent of bronze" (Numbers 21:9) and sticks it on a pole. When the people look at this serpent (or snake, but "serpent' sounds more formal), they live. In John 3:14, Jesus refers to this incident.

Genesis also tells us that the snake is both "more crafty" and is one of the wild animals "that the Lord God had made." The Hebrew term "crafty," *'arum*, is a cognate of the term for "naked" (*'arumim*). We could say that the snake told the woman the "naked truth." Save for the translation here of "crafty," the other places where *'arum* appears in the Bible suggest cleverness or prudence. Proverbs 12:16 reads, "Fools show their anger at once, / but the prudent (*'arum*) ignore an insult." I would like to be known as "prudent", and I think I'd like to be known as "clever": I'm not so sure about "crafty" (unless it has to do with knitting).

The snake is a "wild animal" (the Hebrew literally means "animal of the field," which can be distinguished from a domesticated animal). It could have been one of the creatures paraded before the human being in search of a partner. Finally, the snake is one of God's creations, just as is the human being. The point puts an end to any speculation that the snake could be divine or another god, as it was in other ancient cultures. Our snake is just a snake—it's not a god, it's not immortal, and it's not Satan, although at this point it is a snake that can walk and talk.

God put the forbidden fruit in the garden; God made the snake. It appears to me that God wants the human being(s) to move from innocence to maturity, to move out of the garden and into the world.

The snake asks the woman, "Did God say, 'You shall not eat from any tree in the garden'?" (3:1b). We can speculate as to why the snake doesn't chat up the man: Did he think the man or the woman the more intelligent one? Did he figure that construction from bone and flesh is more aware than construction from dirt? Did he think he could make better headway with the woman, since she did not receive the instruction about the tree from God directly (the instruction comes before her creation)? We can also speculate as to the snake's investment in this drama. Did it (or, since Hebrew is a gendered language with male and female but not neuter, "he") want the fruit for himself, given that snakes are associated with immortality? Was the snake interested in challenging God, but indirectly (from this idea, we eventually get to the idea, much later than Genesis, that the snake was Satan)? Was the snake interested in helping the humans to greater maturity?

The snake's question cleverly misstates what God said and so sets up the woman in the role of correcting a mistaken view. She responds that God permitted fruit from any tree in the garden, but concerning the "tree that is in the middle of the garden," the man and woman are neither to eat its fruit or "touch it" or they'll die (3:2-3). That the tree of life is in the middle of the garden goes unnoted. Of greater concern here is the comment about touching the tree. Perhaps the man told her not to touch the tree to emphasize its forbidden nature. Perhaps she added this prohibition. If so, was this a good move (she is enhancing the word of God by interpretation and application, as for example, Jesus extends the commandment against murder to a commandment against being angry) or a bad move (she is adding to God's word, as if it were insufficient)? Our answer will likely depend on whether we think of the woman as admirable or in the wrong. I choose team-woman here, but I can see reasons to choose otherwise.

There's a midrash that depicts the snake as pushing the woman so that she touches the tree. When she doesn't die, the snake can affirm that the threat of death is not real. The push is not needed because the snake already has an effective rhetorical counter. He tells the woman that if she eats the fruit, she will not die. To the contrary, "God knows that when you eat of it your eyes will be opened, and you will be like God, knowing good and evil" (3:5). The better translation of the Hebrew is "you will be like gods" (plural, that is, the heavenly court). The woman has options: spend her life naked in a garden planting seeds and pulling weeds or being like gods, which sounds like a good option. People may want to be gods, as we saw at Babel. For Genesis, our task is to be human, to learn from our failures, to realize that actions have consequences, and to develop resilience. The woman can believe the man, who likely conveyed the dietary instructions to her, or she can believe the snake. Had the text reported any conversation between the woman and the man, other than his calling her "this," I'd have been more optimistic about her listening to him.

The woman considers the snake's claim. She observes that "the tree was good for food" (nonpoisonous, nutritious, probably loaded with vitamin C and antioxidants), "it was a delight to the eyes" (aesthetically pleasing), and most important, it "was to be desired to make one wise" or to grant understanding (brain food!). She eats. She wants to be like gods, and why not? Gods are immortal; gods are powerful; gods are in the heavenly court. Gods are like kings, only better, and to quote both Mel Brooks and Tom Petty, "It's good to be king!" The Wise Woman of Tekoa (we'll meet her again in the chapter on Cain and Abel) butters up King David by saying, "for my lord the king is like the angel of God, discerning [lit. "hearing"] good and evil... my lord has wisdom like the wisdom of the angel of God to know all things that are on the earth" (2 Samuel 14:17, 20).

She eats. I do not know whether she realized what had happened as soon as she tasted the fruit and wanted the man to experience her new status with her. She also gives some to her man (NRSVue "husband"), and he eats (3:6). I do not see where she has done anything wrong: she had two options, and she made a choice. One was indirect instruction from God; one was direct instruction from one of God's creations. Then again, I was always one to question orders: Why must we do this? Why must we not do that? Children learn, fairly quickly, that the parental and pedagogical response "Because I said so" is not necessarily a good answer.

The man was with her. He could have said, "Sweetie, not a good idea." He could have refused to eat. He could have performed the Heimlich maneuver on her. I do not know whether the man ate because he's operating on automatic, because he trusts her, or because he wants to share whatever happens with her. We can look at him as a hero for willingly transgressing divine instruction to be with her (see 1 Timothy 2:13-14). We can also look at him as a dolt for eating without thinking.

Our decision will depend on whether we think of the man as a concerned and loving husband or as a clod.

The snake, this crafty/prudent creature, did not lie. The human beings do not die a physical death. I'd love to know what the snake is now thinking: Gosh, these human beings are stupid? Oh no, God's going to be angry? Hmmmmm…tasty? We never hear the snake's reaction, and the snake will not speak again.

The human beings do not die; rather, they lose childhood innocence and they move from the realm of nature to the realm of culture: "Then the eyes of both were opened, and they knew that they were naked, and they sewed fig leaves together and made loincloths for themselves" (3:7). Infancy is over; the time when everything is fun is over; the time when we are taken care of is over. Yet there will come for some a second type of infancy. In 2 Samuel 19:35 (19:36 in the [Hebrew] Masoretic text), the loyal advisor Barzillai turns down King David's offer of a home in Jerusalem. He explains, "Today I am eighty years old; can I discern what is pleasant and what is not?" The Hebrew reads, "…can I know [the difference] between good and evil…?" Barzillai knows exactly what he is doing, but he appeals to the problem we will come to call Alzheimer's disease or other forms of dementia.

My mother-in-law, who died this past March, suffered from a relatively mild case of dementia. Her filters were off; she lacked "the knowledge of good and evil" in the sense of what should be said aloud and what thoughts are best kept to oneself. The result of her condition could be embarrassing or extremely funny. She could still communicate, but she was shameless (in a good way). I loved her, and I miss her a great deal.

The first man and woman realize that life has changed. The snake did not lie to them: they have obtained maturity. However, the text does not say that they sinned; the term "sin" first appears in the story of Cain. Whether they "sinned" or not will depend on how we define "sin." Is to disobey a parental warning to "sin" or to assert independence, or both? While the man and woman face the repercussions of their actions, such as being expelled from Eden, God will care for them and go with them outside of Eden.

Deflecting Blame

The couple hears the sound of God walking in the garden. I don't picture God wearing heavy shoes, and a well-tended garden is not likely to have branches to crunch underfoot. I'd like to think God was whistling or perhaps singing, which is what I would be doing if I were walking (alone) in a garden. It's "the time of the evening breeze"; this should be a time of rest and satisfaction, of reflecting on a day well spent. But not this evening.

The man and "his wife" hide themselves from God among the trees. God calls to the man, "Where are you?" (3:9). I am becoming increasingly sympathetic to the woman: God didn't talk to her at the time of her creation; God does not talk to her now. At least the snake paid her some attention. Whether God knows where the couple is hiding and wants them to come out on their own or whether God does not know cannot be determined from the narrative. Later readers, regarding God as omniscient, presume the question is the invitation to accept responsibility. God here reminds me of the parent (I've been in this role) who asks the children with crumbs on their fingers and chocolate on their lips, "Did you eat the cookies I told you to save for after dinner?"

The man responds that he heard the sound of God in the garden and that because he was naked, he was afraid and hid (3:10). Technically, the man was not quite naked: he had a fig leaf. Figs used for houseplants have leaves ranging from four to ten inches; the fiddle-leaf fig has leaves that can be as long as eighteen inches, with a width of a foot. Such a leaf could cover a lot. However, fig leaves can irritate the skin and thus, for various reasons, do not make a great fashion choice.

Then God queries the man how he found out he was naked and whether he had eaten the forbidden fruit—cookie crumbs. God knows, and the man engages in a double deflection: "The woman whom you gave to be with me, she gave me fruit from the tree, and I ate" (3:12). In other words, had God not created the woman, she would not have given him the fruit, and he would not have eaten it. This is the ancient version of "Mom, if you hadn't bought the cookies and pointed them out to me, I would not have eaten them."

The woman has a similar problem with admitting fault. God's first words to her are "What is this that you have done?" It's not an auspicious beginning for a long-term relationship. She partially deflects, "The serpent tricked me, and I ate" (3:13). She could have blamed God, given that the snake was among the wild animals "that God had made." She also could have explained her reasoning and noted, by the way, "We ate, and we are not dead."

God never asks the snake what it thought it was doing or what it wanted, so we'll never know the snake's motives. Instead, God explains the results of their actions.

Life As It Is

God's first and only words to the snake, aside from the "be fruitful and multiply" of Genesis 1, are also not auspicious. The opening comment, "Because you have done this," is vague. Done what? Beguiled the woman or told her the truth? In these days of the whistleblower who is punished rather than rewarded, I'm sympathetic to the snake. Not all people who do the right thing or speak the truth are rewarded. In various ways, truth comes with consequences. God curses the snake: it will now crawl on its belly and eat dust (3:14). This is what infants do as they start becoming mobile: most babies crawl before they walk. Babies learn to talk, but the snake will lose this power. As the man and the woman move from infancy to maturity, the snake regresses.

Next, God sets up an antipathetic relationship between snakes and humanity: the humans will seek to kill snakes (they "will strike your head"), and snakes will reciprocate ("and you will strike [their] heel" [3:15]). Herpetologists, people who study ectothermic tetrapods (i.e., reptiles and amphibians) and, in particular, aphidologists, people who study snakes, do not find such enmity. They, too, recover part of the garden of Eden.

God's comments to the woman and the following notices to the man are not curses. The man and woman are not "cursed." Rather, they receive details on the consequences of their actions. When we tell children, including teenagers, "don't do this," we are generally not issuing "commandments": we are providing instruction. When the child acts contrary to our instructions, we do not love the child less and we do not curse the child (although we may utter a curse word), but we make clear the repercussions. Boundaries are usually designed to protect, and yet to test boundaries can be a sign of health and maturity.

Regarding the woman, what God says depends on which translation we read. In the NRSVue, God tells the woman, "I will make your pangs in childbirth exceedingly great; / in pain you shall bring forth children, / yet your desire shall be for your husband, / and he shall rule over you" (3:16a). This translation is redundant. Great "pangs in childbirth" and "in pain shall you bring forth children" is not poetic; the second stanza adds nothing to the first. This translation is also inconsistent. When the same word appears in two juxtaposed statements, different translations are not warranted. The Hebrew terms translated here as both "pangs" and "in pain" is *etzev*, which means "toil" or "labor." For the next verse, God's comments to the man, the NRSVue reads, "...cursed is the ground because of you; / in toil (*etsev*) you shall eat of it all the days of your life" (3:17). I do not see why for women the term is "pain" and for man the term is "toil."

The point, at least as I read these words, is not pain in childbirth, which is going to happen anyway. It is the ongoing physical labor, not only the work of pregnancy and childbirth, but also childcare, along with the women's need to provide for the economic success of the household through cooking and cleaning, making clothes and pots, and so on. Fairly literally, the verse reads, "Multiplying I will multiply your labors and your conceptions (of children); with labor/toil you will bear children" (author translation). Women who hold jobs outside the home and also do all the housework and the childcare get the point.

God's statement is not an assertion of the way things must be, any more than the statement about a man leaving his father and mother favors the husband's relocation. Rich women may not have this second shift, as they can afford hired help or enslaved individuals (even today, with legal slavery in some countries and human trafficking in others) to care for the children and the home. Some do not work at all, whether because they have inherited wealth or because their spouse provides the needed income. But Genesis 3:16 reminds us that not all women have such privilege and that the "second shift" many women face remains an unfair burden placed upon them.

God then tells the woman, "Yet your desire shall be for your husband, / and he shall rule over you" (3:16b). The term for desire shows up two other times in the text, and the uses show its various aspects. Desire can be a negative, as in a craving or an insatiable urge. In the next chapter, God tells Cain, "If you do not do well, sin is lurking at the door; its desire is for you, but you must master it" (4:7). Cain fails to master sin, with its unquenchable desire, and as a result, Cain kills his brother Abel. On the other hand, desire, especially when it is matched by a reciprocal yearning, can be gorgeous. In Song of Songs 7:10, the woman exults, "I am my beloved's, / and his desire is for me." She and Sarah (see Genesis 18:12) would have much to talk about.

Because of this desire, women will continue to produce children, despite the physical and emotional costs, and despite the high mortality rate in antiquity for both mothers and children. As we move through Genesis, we learn that Jacob's beloved wife Rachel dies in childbirth (35:18-19).

There is one more cost to this situation of the second shift and the desire that may work against the woman's physical and mental health. God's comments to her end with the statement, "and he shall rule over you" (3:16c). The phrase could refer to the man's prevailing over her economically: because she has the home-based duties as well as pregnancy, childbirth, and lactation, he has more freedom to earn more money. The one who brings in more income often has the greater say in how it is spent. Again, this is not how things *need* to be, any more than women *need* to experience pain in childbirth (we have medical advances to help with such matters), to earn less than their husbands, or to work the second shift. How things are need not be how things must be. And the text tells us that even if the woman's situation is not one we today face, or even all readers in antiquity faced (e.g., those seven hundred princesses in Solomon's harem), some women do face domestic difficulties, and they deserve our attention and our aid.

Finally, God tells the man, "Because you have listened to the voice of your wife . . ." (3:17). Listening to one's wife should not be the beginning of a curse. In Genesis 21:12, God tells Abraham, "Whatever Sarah says to you, do as she tells you." Nor, by the way, did the man "listen" to his wife because, as far as the narrator is concerned, she said nothing to him. I doubt she wiggled her hips and said, "Come here, big boy." Had she told him about her process of discernment, I can see where the man might have easily listened to her reasoning.

God specifies that because the man ate the forbidden fruit, the ground will be cursed. He will now produce crops with labor (that same Hebrew term, *etzev*). Agricultural farming is not the same thing as gardening for pleasure; work in arable soil is different than plowing through rocks; growing fruit in a garden well-watered by a local river (2:10) is a pleasure; attempting to grow fruit in a rain-dependent area during a drought or a plague of insects or a fire is both backbreaking and heartbreaking.

God concludes by telling the man that he will labor "until you return to the ground (*ha'adamah*), / for out of it you were taken; / you are dust, / and to dust you shall return" (3:19). The ground that will prove unyielding, bringing out thorns and thistles, will also be the final resting place.

Yet the story has hope. Isaiah 11:8 speaks of a time when the harsh conditions are alleviated, when "the nursing child shall play over the hole of the asp, / and the weaned child shall put its hand on the adder's den." This reversal of the enmity between the woman's children and the snake is also a time when, as the next verse states, "They will not hurt or destroy / on all my holy mountain, / for the earth will be full of the knowledge of the Lord."

Human beings are not merely dust or dirt; we are not only flesh and bone. We are also imbued with the "breath of life" (2:7). We may have lost immortality, or at least the chance of it, but we can gain immortality through our children and through what we contribute to the world for better or ill. Some of us may anticipate resurrection of the flesh or immortality of the soul, since the biblical story begins with

Genesis, but it does not end there. We are destined to fill the earth and care for it. We are in the image and likeness of the divine. The wise compilers of Genesis have given us options, and we can choose which to emphasize.

Exile—or Emancipation

The chapter ends not with death, but with hope. Following the curse of the ground, the man "named his wife (or 'woman') Eve because she was the mother of all living" (3:20). The Hebrew beneath the name Eve is *chavah*, which is a cognate to the Hebrew word for "life." God issues a death sentence, "You are dust," and the man responds with courage and resilience by choosing life. His naming of the woman could indicate possession, but it can also be taken as an affirmation that now the woman (*ishah*) is no longer just a part of the man (*ish*). She is her own person, with a distinct name. She achieves immortality through the generations, as "all living" can trace themselves back to her.

I'd like to think that in response to the man's reaction, God reacts in kindness as well. "The LORD God made garments of skin for the man and his wife (woman) and clothed them" (3:21). We do not know the details of this skin (one rabbinic commentary suggests that the garments were made of the skin that the snake sloughed off, which, like the fig leaf, also seems itchy to me). The notice also signals that humans and animals have a new relationship. While humans do not yet eat meat, the animal now fulfills the (new) human need for clothing. The change in humanity's knowledge, and so the rise of culture, creates a change in our relationship to the animal world. Woolen garments do not harm the sheep; garments of leather and fur typically require the death of the animal. Things are changing, and Genesis suggests that we stop and think about the sources of our food and our clothes.

Later texts will demonstrate how clothing, a mark of distinction between humans and animals and a sign of civilization, can deceive. The next appearance of "skins" is Genesis 27:16, where Rebekah puts goatskin on the hands of her son Jacob so that he can deceive his father. The next use of the term for "garment" is in Genesis 37:3, where Jacob gives his son Joseph a special garment (NRSVue "ornamented robe"), the same garment Joseph's brothers will strip off him, dip in blood, and present to Jacob as (false) evidence that his beloved son had been mauled by a wild beast. Clothing can be a marker of maturity and a guard against shame; it cannot, however, ultimately cover up shameful actions. It can protect; it can also deceive.

Next, God remarks to the heavenly court, "The humans have become like one of us, knowing good and evil..." (3:22). The snake was right! The humans are no longer innocent children; they have not only achieved maturity, but they have also awakened to sexual awareness. That the man named his wife "mother of all living" suggests that both men and women are, well, aware of the birds and the bees.

God sends them out of Eden and blocks the garden's entrance with "the cherubim and a sword flaming and turning to guard the way to the tree of life" (3:24). The expulsion is practical: had humans lived forever, the world would be overpopulated in just a few generations. The ancient world was aware of overpopulation. The *Enumah Elish* describes the gods as complaining about how noisy human beings had become: The noise is the prompt for this Ancient Near Eastern flood story.

I take the expulsion as a good thing for other reasons as well. Life in the well-watered, lush garden is not necessarily an ideal setting. Genesis 13:10 describes the "plain of Jordan" as "well watered everywhere like the garden of the LORD"; it sounds ideal until the verse ends with the notice, "This was before the LORD destroyed Sodom and Gomorrah." Any paradise can become a hell, given free will and the maturity that comes with it, including competition for resources.

We are dust, but we are also in the divine image. Unlike the snake and the ground, we are not cursed. We are human, but we can achieve immortality through our contributions to life. Since our time is limited, we are better prepared to make the most of it. We are no longer in the garden, where work is easy, and there are no challenges; we are in the world that we make, of textiles and pottery, art and music, of making a home and finding ways of creating joy. We are not gods, and I think that's a good thing. Too much power is too much of an opportunity for corruption.

While rabbinic tradition understands Adam and Eve as modeling repentance, and Christian tradition locates in Eden the "original sin" that all of Adam's descendants inherit, Genesis 2–3 makes neither point explicit. This story of human origins is one view of how things came to be—the difficulties of life, the extra work mothers have, the concern to find the person who completes us, and the difficulties such relationships create; it is not prescriptive of how things must be. If I had a choice between wisdom and immortality, I'd opt for wisdom. Proverbs 3:18 wisely states of Wisdom, "She is a tree of life to those who lay hold of her; / those who hold her fast are called happy."

CHAPTER 2

Cain and Abel

Adam and Eve show no indication of repentance, although later Jewish tradition sees them as both modeling repentance and resulting in divine forgiveness. Repentance requires maturity; it is more difficult to recognize that we have done something wrong than to regret having been caught. How parents model the ability to disagree calmly, engage in healthy responses to disappointments, and practice encouragement and patience can help their children deal with life's inevitable difficulties.

The story of Cain and Abel, the world's first children, lacks information on parenting. I wonder what, if anything, Adam and Eve could have done to help Cain through his frustrations, or perhaps to help Abel model support and humility. The story of the first two brothers is also a story of sacrifice, divine mercy, survival, and memory. Through it, we can explore and then provide our own moral interpretations of matters such as the price of free will, the source of sin, and appropriate responses to criminal action where someone gets hurt.

Two Sons

Adam and Eve, having eaten the fruit from the tree of the knowledge of good and evil, became like gods [NRSVue "like God"] knowing good and evil" (3:5). They know that they are naked, and so they have awareness of shame. They learn there are consequences for disobeying God's instructions, although I do not know whether they have an awareness of sin, which is not always easy to define. Ignoring the advice of a parent, or a dissertation director, does not usually fall in the "sin" category. How we think of sin will have something to do with how we understand God: as a loving parent seeking to guide us but recognizing our free will, or as a disciplinarian with belt in hand and ready to punish. I'm inclined toward the first option.

Genesis 4 opens with the notice, "The man [Hebrew *ha-'adam*] knew his wife Eve, and she conceived and bore Cain." It is also possible, because Hebrew verb tenses are notoriously difficult to determine, that Cain or even Cain and Abel were both conceived in and born in Eden. Sexual contact does not require a knowledge of good and evil, as the animal world shows. But I like the idea that post-Eden, the couple not only appreciated physical intimacy but came together in love. When the term "know" is used in relation to conception, the knowledge involved is not a matter of Mensa or Phi Beta Kappa. This knowing suggests an emotional connection that surfaces between two adults and is different than the connection between an infant and a loving caregiver.

I also like the idea that *she*, the woman, did the conceiving, especially since her name (Hebrew *chavah*) comes from the root meaning "life." She is the one who brings new life. It will take biologists another two millennia to discover that conception is substantially a maternal process, with the ovum determining which of the three million or so blind sperm to accept.

We can understand this conception as a form of obedience or compliance, as the first couple has started the process of being fruitful and multiplying (1:28). But much more is going on than assent to this initial instruction. An alternative to personal immortality, lost when the tree of life cannot be accessed, is to live on through the next generation.

I would have liked some comment on how Eve felt about this pregnancy, or whether the deliveries were easy, or how she is now feeling about Adam, but this is a patriarchal text.

Eve names her child (about half of the biblical notices about naming attribute the act to the mother) Cain, a pun on the Hebrew *qanah*, meaning "to get" or "to receive." She states, "I have produced (*qaniti*) a man with (NRSVue: the help of) the LORD" (4:1). "Lord" here is the Hebrew *YHWH*, the name of God. Thus, Eve is the first person in the Bible to utter the sacred name! The addition of "with the help of" is misleading, since the Hebrew here says nothing about "help." There is no allusion here to the woman's role as the man's "helper" (2:18, 20). The Hebrew can be read as "with God." Adam slept while God took his *tzela* and created a woman, so now Eve attributes this ability to create a human being to herself and God. Good for her.

Later interpretation suggests that Eve and the snake were more than conversation partners and that the snake was not just a reptile but was Satan himself. From the New Testament, 1 John 3:10-12 distinguishes between the "children of God" and the "children of the devil" and elaborates, "We must not be like Cain, who was from the evil one and murdered his brother. And why did he murder him? Because his own deeds were evil and his brother's righteous." This explanation presumes that paternity determines actions. It does not. Calling people children of the devil is unhelpful: It dehumanizes them and robs them of their divine image. It also gives them too much power in that it attributes supernatural abilities to them.

On a more positive note, the naming of Cain may be an etiology for the "Cainites" or Kenites (see, e.g., Genesis 15:19; Judges 1:16; 4:11; 1 Samuel 30:29); semitic cognates of this term suggest "metalworker" or, for a more common surname, "Smith." Tubal-cain, whom we meet in Genesis 4:22, is known for working in bronze and iron—a striking note, since the Iron Age only begins in the period of the Judges.

My takeaways at this point: first, children sometimes inherit traits—for music, art, engineering, etc.—but they need to be taught to share, to have compassion, to respect themselves and others. Second, Cain works in agriculture, and his descendants work with metal from the earth. Although the earth does not yield its resources easily, it serves as the source of food and of metal. What appears to be cursed can also be a blessing. Whether the food will be hoarded or shared or whether the metal will be for swords or for plowshares are other questions.

"Next," we are told, Eve bore Cain's "brother Abel" (4:2a). Here, there is no reference to God or to Adam. Again, the Bible omits details I'd like to know: How many years passed between the births? Was one child out of diapers by the time the second arrived—indeed, were there diapers?

I am also intrigued by Abel's identification: "his brother," not "Eve's second son." Genesis 4 sets up the motif of rival siblings: Ishmael and Isaac, Esau and Jacob, Leah and Rachel, Joseph and his (older) brothers, Aaron and Moses, the prudent son and the prodigal son of Luke 15. Biblical accounts tend to prefer the younger son. Simplistic readings cast the older as the villain and the younger as the hero. But the Bible is not a simplistic text. The story of Cain and Abel also sets up a pattern of sympathy for the older siblings. Their concerns are not trifles; their responses are understandable; and our reactions should be sympathetic, not condemnatory.

Abel's name receives no explanation, but the Hebrew *hevel* suggests something like ephemerality, emptiness, or futility. The lack of explanation matches the meaning of the name. The same term, *hevel*, appears in Ecclesiastes 1:2, the famous "vanity of vanities." With a closer connection to Genesis 4, Psalm 144:4 describes humans, "They are like a breath; / their days are like a passing shadow." While God told the first humans that they are dust and will return to dust (Genesis 3:19), no one has died yet. But now we realize that Abel's death has been foreshadowed.

Abel's name reminds me of the names of the sons of Elimelech and Naomi in the Book of Ruth: Chilion and Mahlon, respectively meaning "sickly" and "frail." Why would parents saddle children with such names? Perhaps Eve, who was told she would bear children "along with labor" (see chapter 1), realized that a second child would make life twice as difficult. I imagine Eve suffering postpartum depression.

I also wonder whether Adam lent a gentle hand to the raising of his children. Cain is following in his father's footsteps, for Adam was also an agriculturalist. While God told Adam that "in toil you shall eat of [the food that you grow from the ground] all the days of your life" (3:17), he now has Cain to help him. Did Adam take Cain's help for granted? Did Cain resent having to go into the family business while Abel herded sheep? And who helped Abel?

Job Descriptions

"Abel was a keeper of sheep (literally, a "shepherd of sheep"; the Hebrew does not suggest "keeper" in the sense of Cain's "Am I my brother's keeper?"), and Cain a tiller of the ground" (4:2b). The better translation here is "a servant of the ground." This is the role of the human: to serve the ground (see Genesis 2:5, 15; 3:23). "Till" doesn't have, for me, the sense of serving. The text's favoring of the younger son over the older is hinted at in the listing: Abel, the younger, comes first, and so by implication will his animal sacrifice.

Abel, the shepherd, has dominion over the animals, as God suggested back in Genesis 1:26. As a shepherd, he anticipates Rachel (29:6, 9), Jacob (30:31), Joseph (37:2), Moses (Exodus 3:1), and David (1 Samuel 16:11; 17:34), among others. Psalm 23 gloriously proclaims, "The Lord is my shepherd." In the Gospel of John (10:11), Jesus announces that he is the "good shepherd," and rabbinic sources portray the great Rabbi Akiva, killed by the Romans about a century after Jesus, as a shepherd.

Commentators in previous generations spoke glowingly of the life of the shepherd, in the fields, communing with nature. They likely had images of Louis XIV and his court prancing on the grounds of Versailles. Or we heard that the ancient Israelites more highly valued the shepherd (the pastoral nomad) over the agriculturalist (the city dweller) because shepherds were less interested in private property, more communal, and less likely to enslave. This, too, is romanticization. Herders can be socially stratified, with some having bigger tents or larger flocks. Home-dwellers can work together. We could just as easily suggest that ancient Israel valued herders more than agriculturalists because a good steak tastes better, even smells better, than Brussels sprouts.

Today, it is common to read in Christian commentaries that shepherds were unclean or despised, and it is to these "nobodies" that the angels announced the birth of Jesus. This view is also incorrect. Shepherds at the time of Jesus were not seen as marginal or outcasts. If they were, no one would have paid attention to them when they announced Jesus's birth (Luke 2:7-8). Shepherding is a responsible job that requires skill and courage,

However, I am wary of the metaphor of the "shepherd-leader." I'm not thrilled with the idea of congregations as a flock, or as sheep; "muttonhead" is not a compliment, and the image of a sheep as a victim ("like a lamb led to the slaughter") is not encouraging.

A final note about Abel the shepherd: for the church fathers, he is a prefiguration of Christ. He is a good shepherd, as Jesus is a Good Shepherd (see John 10). He dies, as Jesus dies. His blood speaks, as the blood of Jesus speaks. Such prophetic allegories can be helpful; they can also lead down dangerous paths. Augustine's *City of God* (15.7) epitomizes the problem. Not only does Augustine see Abel as symbolizing Christ, but he also sees Cain as symbolizing the Jews who, according to Augustine, killed Christ. Supporting this reading is Matthew 23:35, where Jesus tells the scribes and Pharisees: "Upon you may come all the righteous blood shed on earth, from the blood of righteous Abel to the blood of Zechariah son of Barachiah, whom you murdered between the sanctuary and the altar." Some Christians came to see biblical older brothers (Cain, Ishmael, Esau) as the Jews, evil figures to be replaced by the beloved younger brothers (Abel, Isaac, Jacob) representing Christianity. This is neither a necessary nor a helpful reading.

The Sacrifice

Without explanation, "in the course of time Cain brought to the LORD an offering of the fruits of the ground (Hebrew *'adamah*, the arable soil) and Abel for his part brought of the firstlings of his flock, their fat portions" (4:3-4a). We do not know how they came to know "the LORD" (*YHWH*), or what sort of relationship they had. Did God walk in the cool of the evening with them? Did they get details from their parents?

Nor do we know why they decided to make offerings. The prompt may be thanksgiving for successful harvests and productive flocks, sunshine, and water. It may be a desire for protection: please let the good weather continue and protect us from drought and disease. It may be a desire to share, since sacrificing is a sharing between God and humanity. The Hebrew term for Cain's offering is *mincha*, better translated "gift." It is the technical term for the grain or cereal offering (when I first heard this term, when I was a child, I thought cereal offerings concerned corn flakes) presented in the Jerusalem Temple; after the Romans destroyed the Temple in 70 CE, it came to refer to the Sabbath afternoon synagogue service.

This lack of motive raises the broader question of sacrifice. For example, today, what might "sacrifice" convey? Is the death of Abel or Jesus or a martyr a "sacrifice"? Is a donation to a religious or political institution a sacrifice? If we sacrifice a pawn or lay down a sacrifice bunt, do we do so for a greater good? Do we assess a sacrifice by its size, value, or the percentage of income it represents?

Then the shocker: "The LORD had regard (better, "respect") for Abel and his offering, but for Cain and his offering he had no regard" (4:4b-5a). My first question, on the practical level, is how one would know. I doubt there was a rating score, with grain offerings getting a 5.5 and meat offerings a 6.0. We could import later biblical materials, where God sends down fire from heaven to accept an offering. For example, concerning the prophet Elijah's sacrifice designed to tell the people "that you, O LORD, are God and that you have turned their hearts back," 1 Kings 18:38 reports: "Then the fire of the LORD fell and consumed the burnt offering, the wood, the stones, and the dust and even licked up the water that was in the trench." Other examples of such divine reception include Leviticus 9:24 (for Moses and Aaron), Judges 6:21 (for Gideon), and 2 Chronicles 7:1 (for King Solomon). Perhaps Cain "felt" that something was off. Ritual does not always produce the appropriate emotional response. Or perhaps I've been overthinking.

God chooses Abel's sacrifice over Cain's, but the text gives no reason for the preference. The ancient rabbis suggested that Abel's "firstlings" meant the best portion, whereas Cain did not take the best fruits. There may also be a practical difference. Cain offers agricultural produce, something he could have eaten himself. Abel offers animal products, but the people of the time are still vegetarian. Thus, Cain offers what is of more value, as he offers something he can use. The Epistle to the Hebrews (11:4) offers (couldn't resist the pun), "By faith Abel offered to God a more acceptable (lit. "greater") sacrifice than Cain's. Through this he received approval as righteous, God himself giving approval to his gifts; he died, but through his faith (lit: "it") he still speaks."

Explanations seeking to make sense of the text may not be needed. The point may be that the choice is arbitrary, a mark of God's free will. God says to Moses, "I will be gracious to whom I will be gracious and will show mercy on whom I will show mercy" (Exodus 33:19). We should not treat our relationship with the divine as if it worked on automatic: we go through the appropriate rituals, recite the right prayers, and make generous donations, and therefore God will reciprocate in kind with lottery wins, job offers, and remission of disease. God loves us, but combinations of free will, science (the way the world and our bodies work), and happenstance also have roles to play.

Finding a reason to justify divine choice is comparable to finding a reason to justify unfairness. Searching for answers—for why our sacrifice, our offering, our best effort, etc., was not accepted—can create more problems. It can make us feel inadequate; it can encourage us to offer more and more and so impoverish ourselves even as frustration and resentment set in. People who pray for miracles may think, if I had more faith, then my father would not have died, I would not have lost my job, the flood would not have destroyed my home, and so on. The Bible is brutally honest: sometimes the world is not fair. Bad things happen to good people. The better question may be not "Why did this happen?" but "What do I do now?"

Realizing that God disregarded ("disrespected" or even "dissed") his sacrifice, "Cain was very angry" (4:5b). I don't blame Cain. While the text does not tell us *why* Cain was angry, explanations are not difficult to find. Cain could have been angry at himself: he did not give the best that he had; what he gave was insufficient. He could have been angry with, or jealous of, Abel. He could have been angry with God for what he perceived to be an arbitrary judgment.

Righteous anger, the anger that we feel when we perceive an injustice, strikes me as a good thing. But anger needs to be channeled for it to be anything more than a problematic way of burning calories. I recall a song by Aerosmith, "Don't Get Mad, Get Even." I'm not happy with this either. Rather than getting mad or even, we are better off doing something constructive.

Verse 4:5 ends by telling us that Cain's "countenance fell," or he was "crestfallen." Not too many of my friends speak about their "countenances" these days, and fewer would speak about being crestfallen. The Hebrew literally says, "His face fell." We can picture the sides of his mouth turning downward, his forehead creasing in a frown, his eyes narrowing, his nostrils flaring. Because the word translated "became angry" can also mean "became hot," we can also picture him turning ruddy as blood rushes to his face. Or we can see him as both angry and depressed and so unable to lift his head. Moving from the literal description to the theological implication: when one's face falls, one moves away from being in the divine image and likeness.

God's Response

Like a good teacher (I'm projecting), God recognizes that Cain did not take the news of his failed sacrifice well. It would have been better had Cain asked why the sacrifice was rejected (it would have been better had Adam and Eve asked a few more questions about those trees in the garden), but at least God notices. God asks Cain, "Why are you angry, and why has your countenance (lit. "face") fallen?" (4:6). Back to Eden: "Did you eat from the tree?" God knows the answer, but God wants Cain to put his feelings into words.

God then, enigmatically, says, "If you do well, will you not be accepted? And if you do not do well, sin is lurking at the door; its desire is for you, but you must master it" (4:6-7). The more literal translation does not help much. The Hebrew reads, "Is it not that if you do good, that it will be lifted, and if you do not do good, by the opening sin is crouching, and upon you is its desire [i.e., you are the one it desires], but you are able [or 'shall' or 'must'] to rule over it." Oy. Even the Talmud (*b. Yoma* 52a-b) notes that the Torah has five verses whose meaning cannot be securely determined. Geneses 4:7 is the first example (the others, for another time, are Exodus 25:34 on ark decoration; Exodus 17:9 on the time to fight the enemy; Genesis 49:7 on what is cursed, and Deuteronomy 31:16 on resurrection).

Here's my take. The first part, "Is it not that if you do good, that it will be lifted," means that it is our own reaction that is of import. We can be lifted up by our reactions to disappointment: I handled that well; I took that as a learning opportunity; I am not going to let my anger determine how I shall proceed; I am not going to belittle myself through jealousy. The idea of being lifted up nicely counters the image of the fallen face or the depressed reaction.

The second part of the verse hints at what our reaction should be: "If you do not do good, by the opening sin is crouching, and upon you is its desire, but you are able to [or 'can' or 'must'] rule over it." We can rise above the occasion (to continue the "lifting up" idea), or we can lower ourselves into the muck.

Genesis 4:7 is the Bible's first mention of "sin." Sin is "crouching": the technical term for this depiction is *hypostasis*, the personification of an abstract concept. "Sin" has a "thingness," a palpable reality, to it. "Crouching" suggests a lion ready to maul. Sin has the quality of the predator. Like a lion, it may well be stronger and faster than we are. But we can master it, or we can tame it. In the New Testament, 1 Peter 5:8 warns, "Discipline yourselves; keep alert. Like a roaring lion your adversary the devil prowls around, looking for someone to devour." There are temptations all around, but we can master them.

Other biblical depictions of sin include a weight or burden that can be lifted off (see Psalm 38:4), a stain to be washed away (Isaiah 1:18), or a debt forgiven (this last example, with the remedy of forgiveness, reinforces the connection of debt to sin; see Matthew 6:12, "Forgive us our debts").

Sin needs defining—then and now (it's a good exercise where pronouncements of forgiveness of sins are made to define what is being forgiven and by whom). In its initial context in Genesis 4, sin is acting in anger in a way that does harm (unrighteous anger) rather than channeling it into correctly addressing its source. Sin can be seen as the opposite of the good with which creation started, and it can be mastered. As human beings, we may be inclined to sin. Genesis 6:5 observes that "every inclination of the thoughts of their hearts was only evil continually." But we can resist the evil inclination

God advises Cain that while sin—better, *Sin*, with a capital *S*, an active agent—seeks to master him, Cain can, should, must, master it: "Its desire (*teshuqah*) is for you, but you must master (*timshal*) it." The same two terms appear in 3:16 where God tells the woman, "Your desire (*teshuqah*) shall be for your husband, and he shall rule (*yimshal*) over you." Desire can be human and good or demonic and bad. Mastery or control can be a negative form of coercion, but it can also be a positive form of constraint. Desire in 3:16 is well-directed because it can lead to wanted children and a mutually supportive relationship. But the desire predicated of sin seeks only to devour more and more, since sinful desire is never quenched. Once we are mastered by sin, we are never satisfied.

Cain has a choice: he can do evil and fall into sin's trap, or he can do good and avoid the threat. The Jewish philosopher Maimonides interpreted this verse to mean that repentance lies within Cain's power and that when Cain repents, God will forgive him.

Cain is not totally depraved. He, like all of us, has a choice. Amos 5:14-15 provides a helpful intertext: "Seek good and not evil, / that you may live, / and so the Lord, the God of hosts, will be with you. . . . / Hate evil and love good, / and establish justice in the gate." Amos continues by discussing the mourning of farmers, and we can hear Abel's blood in the background. The text poses the question: Do we choose the good for the sake of present reward or a blessed eternity, or do we choose the good because that is the right thing to do?

The Murder

I wish people in the primeval history had asked more questions. Cain could have asked God what sin was, how to recognize it, and what specifically to do when it came calling. He could have asked what the problem was with his sacrifice. Nothing.

God goes away (the text typically has dialogues, not trialogues or conversations among several people at a time) while 4:8 moves the plot along: "Cain said to his brother Abel, 'Let us go out to the field.'" The narrator tells us, "And when they were in the field, Cain rose up against his brother Abel and killed him" (4:8). The verse presents multiple problems, morally and textually.

The Hebrew did not need to describe Abel as "his brother." There isn't an Abel Goldstein or an Abel Murphy down the street (there may not even be a street; this is only the fourth chapter of Genesis). Rather, the narrator emphasizes that Cain is not killing a stranger; he is killing *his brother*. Not only are the two both in the image and likeness of God; they are also in the image and likeness of their parents. They have a biological bond. Moreover, what impacts one necessarily impacts the other, as well as their parents. The verse then repeats "his brother" and so doubles down on both the initial closeness and the tragedy of the rupture. The next verse will repeat "brother" two times more. To kill anyone is to kill a sibling, a member of the family. It is tantamount to killing one-quarter of the world's population. And it is to distort and destroy the image of God, the image both of the perpetrator with a fallen face and the image of the victim, as the corpse decays.

The term "brothers" occurs frequently in the biblical text, and each reference can serve as an intertext and commentary on the brothers in Genesis 4. Here is one hopeful corrective to the motif of fraternal jealousy. In 13:8, Abraham (still named Abram) says to his nephew Lot, "Let there be no strife between you and me and between your herders and my herders, for we are kindred." The Hebrew behind "kindred" is, no surprise, "brothers." Strife among family members affects not only the individuals involved but also the rest of the family and those associated with them.

Verse 4:8 also introduces a text-critical problem (a problem created when ancient manuscripts do not agree) because "Let us go out to the field" is not in the Hebrew. Likely, some ancient scribes thought that the Hebrew, "Cain said to his brother Abel," needed an object: What did Cain say? The reading in the NRSVue has a stronger logical flow; the Hebrew is more suggestive and so more interesting (at least to me). It leaves up to our imagination what Cain might have said to Abel and how he said it: in anger, in a business-like tone, with all the friendliness in the world?

According to one of the earliest interpretations of Genesis, a Jewish-Hellenistic text from ca. the first century BCE known as the Wisdom of Solomon, "But when an unrighteous man departed from her [Lady Wisdom] in his anger, he perished because in rage he killed his brother" (Wisdom 10:3). For this author, we have Wisdom to guide us, and it is our choice as to whether or not to follow her.

One midrash explains that Abel had taunted Cain about his rejected sacrifice, and Cain acted in response to his taunts. This may be an early version of what is called "blaming the victim." It also provides a helpful warning: when we succeed where another fails, we are not to provoke the person whom we bested. Gloating is unattractive. In the Sermon on the Mount (Matthew 5:23-24), Jesus advises, "When you are offering your gift at the altar, if you remember that your brother or sister has something against you, leave your gift there before the altar and go; first be reconciled to your brother or sister, and then come and offer your gift." While the proximate reference concerns Temple sacrifice, there may be a hint of Cain and Abel here: what happens in the field could be the result of a feud long simmering.

Another midrash, found also in Muslim sources, suggests that the brothers fought not about the sacrifice but about Cain's refusal to give Abel his twin sister (who knew?) for a bride. The brothers fought, the devil heard them, and conveniently showed up carrying a stone, which Cain then used to strike Abel.

Yet another reading suggests that Cain and Abel fought over the ownership of the world, which they figured they'd inherit. Here, the fight is over economics and politics. There was more than enough to go around (the world is a big place), but as we've noted, sin is insatiable. Not only does it want more and more, but it also prompts us to want what others have.

One final midrash suggests that the brothers fought over theology. Cain insists, based on God's rejection of his sacrifice, that the world was not created with love and that justice is corrupt. Abel insists that Cain is wrong since his sacrifice was better and so God judged correctly rather than capriciously. Cain rejects the concepts of judgment and a good judge, of an afterlife, of reward for the righteous and punishment for the wicked. Here is a place where conversation is needed. Cain, who has a point, sounds like the modern atheist. Today, many people claim that the enemy of civilization is atheism and, by extension, secularism. Personally, I'm more worried by the fundamentalists in any tradition than the secularists. We can reject ideas of an afterlife or of God but still have a moral compass.

These various interpretations concerning why Cain killed Abel land on the major sources of disagreement today: sex, economics/politics, theology. They also tell us that disagreement can lead to enmity. Be careful: Sin is crouching at the door, and its desire is insatiable. Be careful: Perhaps if Cain had, as we are told in kindergarten, "used his words" and told Abel what the problem was, the murder could have been averted. Be careful: To kill one person is to murder one-quarter of the world's population. To kill is to murder a member of our family, a person also in the divine image.

And be careful—because the Hebrew gives no motive, it also warns against judging. We do not know whether Cain's actions were premeditated; we do not know whether Abel exacerbated a bad situation. We know nothing of how they were raised, or even if they understood death, since until the murder, no one had died. In assessing crimes, or sins, intellectual humility is needed.

The Second Conversation

Then God says to Cain, "Where is your brother Abel?" (4:9a). Again, a question, and again a reference to "brother." We are back to Eden, where after the business with the snake and the tree, God asked "Where are you?" (3:9), "Who told you that you were naked? Have you eaten from the tree of which I commanded you not to eat?" (3:11), and "What is this that you have done?" (3:13).

Where is Abel? Cain responds, "I do not know" (4:9b). I wonder whether Cain knows. The "breath of life" is no longer in Abel, so where did he go? Cain knows where the body is, but where is Abel? He remains alive in the memory of his parents, of God, and of Cain. Where is Abel? He is in Cain's thoughts and in God's. Cain is his brother's keeper, not only in terms of how we, as human beings, should protect each other, but also in that he cannot escape the memory of his brother and what he did to him.

There are other ways of interpreting Cain's "I do not know." One is that Cain is being snarky. "I don't know" can be read as a cipher for "I don't care" or "Wherever he is, that's irrelevant to me." We can also interpret the Hebrew sentence, normally translated, "I don't know; am I my brother's keeper?" as "I didn't know I am my brother's keeper." Ancient Hebrew lacks punctuation marks, so determining a question from a declarative statement or determining comma placement becomes an art rather than a science.

I suspect Cain's "Am I my brother's keeper?" is another version of deflecting the blame, a response that we saw with Adam's blaming both God and the woman for his eating the fruit. It is easier to turn the tables on the one who accuses us rather than to own up to our own actions.

The term translated "keeper," in Hebrew, *shomer*, connotes keeping not in the sense of taming or locking up (as in lion keeper), or cleaning (as in housekeeper), or following protocols (as in bookkeeper or timekeeper). It means to "guard" or to "watch." It is the same term used 2:15 for God's instruction to the human being regarding care for the garden. It appears again in 3:24 to describe the flaming swords that guard the way back to Eden and so protect it. And it appears again in 17:9, where God tells Abraham, "You shall keep (*shomer*) my covenant, you and your offspring after you throughout their generations." The term for a Jew who refrains from work on the Sabbath (not being on social media, not riding in cars) is *shomer shabbat*, a "guardian" or an "observer" of the Sabbath. The term underlies the name Samaria, and one etymology for the Samaritans is that they are faithful "keepers" of the Torah.

The term *shomer* can even mean "preserve," which makes Cain's question more telling: Am I the one to preserve my brother and keep him from harm? Cain could even be suggesting with his "Am I"—accent on the *I*—that *God* should have protected Abel. God is the *shomer* of Israel who will "bless you and keep (*shomer*) you . . . lift up his countenance upon you and give you peace" (Numbers 6:24-26). According to Psalm 121:7-8, the Lord will "keep you (*shomer*) from all evil; / he will keep (*shomer*) your life. / The LORD will keep (*shomer*) / your going out and your coming in / from this time on and forevermore."

We cannot "love our neighbor," let alone our brothers and sisters, if we do not protect them. The answer to Cain's question is, "Yes, you are your brother's keeper." If we are just for ourselves, asked Rabbi Hillel, who are we? (*Pirke Avot* 1:14). We are to love our neighbor as ourselves (Leviticus 19:18); we are to love the immigrant, since we were immigrants in the land of Egypt (Leviticus 19:34). First John 3:15 proclaims, "All who hate a brother or sister are murderers."

Rather than answering Cain's question, God asks another question: "What have you done? Listen, your brother's blood is crying out to me from the ground!" (4:10). The Hebrew reads "bloods" (plural). The Mishnah (*Sanhedrin* 4:5) draws a legal analogy from the verse: unlike property cases, where repayment is possible, in capital cases, the bloods (plural) indicate unborn descendants: no new children, or children's children, will be born. Murder is thus a crime that includes not only the victim, but the victim's posterity.

The term for "crying" (Hebrew: *tza'aq*) shows up next in Genesis 27:34, when Esau, hearing that his father Jacob had blessed his younger brother, Jacob, "cried out (*tza'aq*) with an exceedingly great and bitter cry and said to his father, 'Bless me, me also, father!'" In Genesis 4, the murdered younger brother's bloods cry out; in the second use, the overlooked older brother cries out. The term reappears multiple times, including Exodus 22:22-23, "You shall not abuse any widow or orphan. If you do abuse them, when they cry out (*tza'aq*) to me, I will surely heed their cry." The various uses of the term remind us that ranking harm—murder is worse than disinheritance is worse than abuse is worse than insult, and so on—is not a helpful exercise. It can place us in the victimization Olympics, where whoever has the worst situation wins. This is not a game I care to play. All causes for distress should be prevented; all distress that we cause because of jealousy or greed or lust should be alleviated.

Genesis 4:10 also raises questions about how we want to see justice done, or even how we understand justice, for the bloods cry *to God*. What would they have God do? What would we have God do? The good news is that God hears the cry of the bloods and so recognizes the need for justice: for Cain to accept the responsibility for what he has done and for Abel to know, somehow, that the assault against him and his posterity will be addressed. Murder cannot go unattended. Justice without mercy is intolerable, but so is mercy without justice.

The bloods cry from the ground, and so the ground is now involved in this first sin. The verse reminds us to ask about the land where we reside. Whose blood was spilled there, and in which war? I am from Massachusetts, which witnessed blood spilled between colonizers and indigenous inhabitants, between the British and the Americans, by religious fanatics and economic profiteers seeking to root out "witches," and by murderers to this day. We live on a blood-soaked earth. The bloods call out, "Remember me." And in that memory, some justice and peace may be found.

The original harmony between humanity and the earth was destroyed by the disobedience of the first man and the first woman. Genesis 4 reverses the curse to focus it on the human being. In Genesis 3:17, God tells the man, "Cursed is the ground because of you; / in toil you shall eat of it all the days of your life." In 4:11, God tells Cain, "Now you are cursed from the ground." The curse has spread from the ground to the human; alienation is working in both directions. The agricultural results are the same. "When you till the ground, it will no longer yield to you its strength" (4:12). God had already told the first man that the work would be one of pain and that the ground would yield thorns and thistles. Matters now devolve.

God continues, "You will be a fugitive and a wanderer on the earth" (4:12). The earth will not yield its strength, and it will not be a home. Once again, what happens in the primeval history is one explanation of how things are, not how things *must* be. We can use agricultural tools and our knowledge of ecology to raise more than thorns and thistles; women can find relief not only from the actual pain of childbearing but also from the sociological second shift. And Cain can find a home.

For a Bible trivia challenge, the question is, "Name a fugitive and a wanderer in the Bible." My first answer would be Cain, but there are other correct responses. Moses is, like Cain, a murderer. Moses is a fugitive from Egypt, and he will wander forty years in the wilderness. Reading Cain in light of Moses, or vice versa, may help us to see each of the men in a different light.

To be a wanderer on the earth is also to make the entire earth one's home. Nomads, travelers, the adventurous among us, are happier with the unsettled life. The story of Cain and Abel, of a family already expelled from the garden of Eden, is a story that asks where one finds a home, of what constitutes that home, and even who might turn a place into a home.

Cain protests: "My punishment is greater than I can bear! Today you have driven me away from the soil, and I shall be hidden from your face; I shall be a fugitive and a wanderer on the earth, and anyone who meets me may kill me" (4:13-14). There is much to unpack here.

First is the familiar issue of translation. The term translated "punishment" in Hebrew is *avon*, a word that can mean "sin." The term is not the same as the "sin" crouching by the door, and it does usually mean "punishment," but I don't want to let the idea of "sin" go. If we read "my sin" or, by extension, "my guilt" is greater than I can bear, then we can see that Cain not only recognizes his responsibility for the murder but also repents from it.

"I can bear" is, in Hebrew, *minso*, from *min*, the preposition meaning "from," and *nasa*, to be lifted up. Thus, "from bearing" or "from being lifted up" is a good translation. However, the expression can also suggest being forgiven, as in a weight that is lifted off one's back or one's shoulders. The medieval Jewish commentator Rashi proposes that Cain asked: "Is my sin too great to be forgiven?" This is a good question. The question places God as the one who must determine whether forgiveness should be granted. I am reminded of one of my insider students at Riverbend Maximum Security Prison in Nashville. In discussing the "unforgivable sin," defined in Matthew 12:31, as "blasphemy against the Spirit," he defined this blasphemy as putting limitations on divine forgiveness or saying "God could not love a man like me."

Next is the question of punishment. This may be the first time Cain has ever been punished. Again, we know nothing of Adam and Eve's parenting skills. Did Cain learn to strike Adam because he was struck by his own parents? Did he see his father strike his mother and know that his mother would later get up and go about as if nothing had happened? Did the brothers hit each other with impunity, without parental correction?

I also find Cain's protest overstated. Abel is dead; his death was more than Cain could bear. On the other hand, I do appreciate Cain's chutzpah: he remains concerned for his own well-being, and he insists that God shares that same concern. His comments also remind me of the expression, "A fate worse than death." This is not a matter on which I'd like to spend time speculating, although Cain may be correct. He will have to deal with what he has done and its repercussions for the rest of his very long life.

As for his being driven from the soil? Not quite. The events in Eden had already created the agricultural problem: nothing changed. Nor is Cain hidden from God's face, any more than his parents could hide themselves in the garden of Eden. The first humans sought to hide themselves from God because they now realized they were naked and that they had ignored God's instruction. Now Cain fears being hidden, even though he, too, is guilty of disobedience. He could have resisted that crouching sin. As for his being a fugitive and a wanderer, Cain rejects the sentence by settling down and building a city (we'll join him there in a few paragraphs). Unlike horror movies, where curses cannot be undone, and the cursed become the victims, in primeval history the curse is the way things seem to be but do not need to be.

Last, Cain fears that he will be killed. "Anyone who meets me"? Who? Early midrashim suggest, as we've seen, that Cain and Abel had twin sisters, thus explaining where Cain found his wife. The "anyone" could be his parents, but that view seems precluded by the report of exile; Cain left his parents. Nor have we any indication that Adam and Eve wanted to kill their son. Cain's fears are human fears, of vulnerability coupled with guilt and, likely, shame.

We can also query why people might want to kill him, and here the role of Cain, the landless refugee, the fugitive and wanderer, comes back into play. Would people seek to harm him because he is a murderer? How would they know? Perhaps they would harm him because he is precisely what God said he would be: a fugitive and a wanderer, a homeless person without a support system. Because he is a stranger (hence the mandate in Leviticus 19:34 to love the immigrant)? Because people are violent, as we see in Genesis 19, the story of Sodom and Gomorrah, and the townspeople's reaction to the two travelers who visit Abraham's nephew Lot?

God assures him, "Not so!" at least in some early translations and, from them, the NRSVue. The Hebrew reads, "Therefore." In the Hebrew, God's assurance that "whoever kills Cain will suffer a sevenfold vengeance" (4:15) can be seen as the *result* of Cain's protestations. Early rabbinic sources interpreted his protests and his desire not to be driven from God's face as repentance. Yet the Hebrew is not clear, so we cannot know whether Cain repented, whether he thought he had done something wrong, or whether he found God just or even trustworthy.

I see irony in God's comment about the "sevenfold vengeance" (keep an eye on this idea, because it will surface as a flood pun in the next chapter on Noah). Death is death, so how this punishment becomes sevenfold remains vague. The deaths of other family members? More, how would the perpetrator know? Cain doesn't have a business card with "sevenfold vengeance if you kill me" embossed on it. Were I Abel, I might be asking about the fairness of this decision: killing Abel gets Cain exiled from a place of exile already, while killing Cain gets a sevenfold vengeance. What is Abel, chopped liver? How is all this death going to stop the killing or teach anyone that killing is not a great way of resolving a problem?

Finally, the narrator states, "The Lord put a mark on Cain, so that no one who came upon him would kill him" (4:15). The comment presumes a universal human language such that anyone, anywhere, would recognize the sign. We can speculate on what the sign looked like—a tattoo, a brand, a scar, a birthmark; according to one midrash, God gave Cain a dog for protection as well as companionship (I'm picturing a labradoodle)—or how it worked.

Signs need interpretation. The bow in the sky is a "sign" that God will not destroy the world again by flood (as discussed in the next chapter), but for some, it is a sign that a pot of gold can be found at its end. Blood on the doorposts of the Israelites is a sign for God to "pass over" that house and not kill the firstborn within it (see Exodus 12:13). Circumcision is the sign of the covenant (someone at some point certainly asked). Thus, Cain would have to explain the sign.

The sign not only signals to outsiders that there is something special about Cain. It is also a reason to ask not simply "Who are you?" but "What does that mark represent?" Cain has a choice of answering: it is a sign of my crime, or it is a sign of divine protection. The sign becomes both a means of protection and, because all signs require interpretation, a means for forming community. Cain's sign asks whether we should be known for the worst thing we have ever done or for the mercy we have been shown. The mark signals to Cain every time he sees his reflection the fact of his crime, the absence of his brother, the need to master sin, and the protection of his God.

The Intertext: When the Bible Comments on Itself

While Cain and Abel do not reappear in Israel's Scripture, their story is retold, and in the retelling, additional nuances occur concerning capital punishment, cursing, justice, and families. According to 2 Samuel 14, Joab, King David's cousin and the head of the army, concocts a ruse with the "Wise Woman of Tekoa" ("Wise Woman" is an office). He tells her to pretend to be in mourning, go to the king, ask for help, and then tell a story: she is a widow with two sons. "They fought with one another in the field; there was no one to part them, and one struck the other and killed him" (2 Samuel 14:6).

The family insists, "Give up the man who struck his brother, so that we may kill him for the life of his brother whom he murdered, even if we destroy the heir as well" (2 Samuel 14:7). In ancient Israel's law code, murder is a capital crime. Exodus 21:12 reads, "Whoever strikes a person mortally shall be put to death." Yet we never see this commandment carried out. Nor are the other capital crimes listed in this chapter shown to be carried out, including the famous "eye for an eye" passage in Exodus 21:24-25. As for "Whoever curses father or mother shall be put to death" (Exodus 21:17), we'd lose more than half of our teenagers if it were put into play. The laws are better seen as legal principles demanding justice, but they do not make clear exactly how it is to be determined or who is responsible for implementing it.

The Wise Woman's story demonstrates how, in executing the perpetrator, the family will be destroyed. As the (faux) widow, with pathos, explains, "Thus they would quench my one remaining ember and leave to my husband neither name nor remnant on the face of the earth" (2 Samuel 14:7). Adam and Eve will have another son, Seth, but the widow will have no more children.

After some back and forth with David, where the king assures the woman that no one will do any harm to her, she gets him to promise, "not one hair of your son shall fall to the ground" (14:11). The protection afforded to the widow's son recollects the protection afforded to Cain, as we will see. To execute the murderer would be to cut off his line from any potential children.

Then the Wise Woman springs her trap: "In giving this decision the king convicts himself, inasmuch as the king does not bring his banished one [Absalom] home again" (14:13). Absalom had killed Amnon, his half-brother and the crown prince. Amnon was not an innocent victim: he had raped Absalom's sister, who was also his half-sister, Tamar. David did nothing, and Absalom used the rape as an excuse to dispatch the crown prince and make a run for David's throne. David had every reason to refuse to reconcile with Absalom. And yet…

Since David forgave the murderer in the widow's story, he should do the same for his own son. The Wise Woman continues: "We must all die; we are like water spilled on the ground, which cannot be gathered up" (14:14a). The image of the spilled water, faintly echoing the image of Abel's blood, is a statement of futility. The water cannot be collected. What is done is done. The verse concludes with the woman's theological observation, "But God will not take away a life; he will devise plans so as not to keep an outcast banished forever from his presence" (14:14b). Cain will not be an outcast from God's presence. No one will. Nor should Absalom be an outcast from David's presence.

After more flattery, the Wise Woman tells David, "My lord the king is like the angel of God, discerning good and evil" (14:17). With this allusion to the story of Adam and Eve and their tasting the fruit from the tree of the knowledge of good and evil, she reminds the king that judgment is now in his hands. He can determine, in this case, who lives and who dies, whether or not he can find reconciliation with his son Absalom.

David figures out that Joab concocted the story of the two sons, and then he orders Absalom's return. Absalom killed his half-brother, the crown prince, David's son. He then began a civil war against his father. Yet when David learns that Absalom had died, he mourns, "O my son Absalom, my son, my son Absalom! Would I had died instead of you, O Absalom, my son, my son" (2 Samuel 18:33).

In light of the woman's story, David's judgment, and then David's mourning, perhaps we might see Cain differently: the son of his mother, not cast out from God. If David can mourn Absalom, perhaps we can feel for Cain. That expression of sympathy, or empathy, is a sign that we are our brother's keeper.

Cain's Legacy

"Cain went away from the presence of the LORD and settled in the land of Nod, east of Eden" (4:16). Well, no, he didn't. The divine presence is everywhere, including the land where Cain and his descendants will settle. That omnipresence is how God knows, two chapters later, what all of humanity is doing. I wonder whether the verse instead indicates that Cain has given up on God. God was the one who refused Cain's sacrifice; God did not stop him from killing his brother; God set the punishment. Cain may want no more to do with God. Alternatively, Cain may not know what to say in the face of divine mercy: rather than striking him dead, God gave Cain a mark of protection. There are times we may want to hide ourselves from God or be away from that divine presence. Anger and resentment may explain why we absent ourselves; feelings of guilt, or not knowing how to reciprocate, or just confusion may also explain our reasons for hiding.

Cain, the one who was to be a fugitive, settles down. The term translated as "Nod" is the Hebrew word for "wanderer," as in "a wanderer (*nod*) and a fugitive." The land, a location known as "wandering," presents a lovely irony: the wanderer settles in Wanderland. "Land of Nod" has come to be a metaphor for "sleep" (as in "nodding off"), which appears in this sense first in the writings of Jonathan Swift.

Despite the curses of alienation, Cain settles down, marries, raises a family, and builds a city. "Cain knew his wife, and she conceived and bore Enoch, and he built a city and named it Enoch after his son Enoch" (4:17). This does not sound like the vagabond life to me.

The text tells us nothing about the wife's genealogy. Various midrashim suggest that she is Abel's twin, which raises questions of her fate: married to the man who killed her brother. If she is Abel's twin, then in a sense Abel lives on in her and in her children. Genesis 5:4 reads, "The days of Adam after he became the father of Seth were eight hundred years, and he had other sons and daughters," so Cain's wife could be another sister. Whether Mrs. Cain was Abel's twin, another of Adam and Eve's children, or a child from another ancient ancestor whose story is not recorded in the Bible cannot be determined. Hers is another story that we readers can imagine.

I'm intrigued by Mrs. Cain, and I'm also intrigued by the city Cain built. Other cities in Genesis are not destination locations. In Genesis 11:4, the people say, "Come let us build ourselves a city and a tower with its top in the heavens"—this is the Tower of Babel. Then there are the cities of Sodom and Gomorrah. Cities, like Jerusalem, can be glorious places. They are also dangerous ones.

The Hebrew word *enoch*, the name of Cain's son and the city, means "dedicated" or "consecrated," although we do not know to what or whom the child was dedicated. This is not the same Enoch to whom the books of Enoch are attributed or about whom we are told, "Enoch walked with God after the birth of Methuselah three hundred years and had other sons and daughters. . . . Enoch walked with God; then he was no more, because God took him" (5:21-24).

Our Enoch, Cain's son, has the much more mundane role of continuing the genealogical line: "To Enoch was born Irad, and Irad was the father of Mehujael, and Mehujael the father of Methushael, and Methushael the father of Lamech" (4:18). The Bible's genealogical lists, which threaten to be mind-numbing (genealogies, like vacation pictures, are usually interesting only if they are ours), then breaks at the seventh generation with Lamech and launches into another story whose details are lost to antiquity. We learn that "Lamech took two wives; the name of the one was Adah, and the name of the other Zillah" (4:19). This is the first notice of polygyny, and it potentially contrasts with Genesis 2:24, the notice that "a man leaves his father and his mother and clings to his wife (singular), and they become one flesh."

Lamech boasts, "Adah and Zillah, hear my voice; / you wives of Lamech, listen to what I say: / I have killed a man for wounding me, / a young man (Hebrew *yeled*, better translated "boy") for striking me. / If Cain is avenged sevenfold, / truly Lamech seventy-sevenfold" (4:23-24). The problem with mercy shown in one generation, such as God's protection of Cain, is that it can be taken as license to harm with impunity in the next generation. Like his ancestor Cain, Lamech kills; unlike Cain, he boasts of killing a child. God had promised Cain that anyone who attacked him would be punished sevenfold. Lamech advances revenge ten times over. He reminds me of Rehoboam, the son of Solomon, in that he thinks he is proportionally greater than his ancestor. Rehoboam takes the advice of his younger (and much less wise) advisors, who tell him to say to the people, "My little finger is thicker than my father's loins" (1 Kings 12:10; this is one of those verses that I like to cite when friends suggest that the Bible should be taught in elementary schools).

Lamech kills when he is struck. Jesus insists, "If anyone strikes you on the right cheek, turn the other also" (Matthew 5:39). Lamech wants to be avenged seventy-sevenfold. When Peter asks Jesus how often he needs to forgive another member of the family gathered in Jesus's name, Jesus responds, "Not seven times, but, I tell you, seventy-seven times" (Matthew 18:22). The Bible asks us good questions about responses to violence. On the one hand, we can resist returning violence with more violence. On the other hand, we risk giving the violent a free pass, and that free pass can encourage them, as it encouraged Lamech, to ratchet up that violence. What do we do with the violent, the murderers, in our communities?

Leviticus 19:18 insists, "You shall not take vengeance or bear a grudge against any of your people"; the next line is "but you shall love your neighbor as yourself." When it comes to determining the just response to injustice, some biblical passages suggest we can rely on God. Deuteronomy 32:43 states that God "will avenge the blood of his children / and take vengeance on his adversaries." Isaiah 61:2 proclaims, "the year of the LORD's favor / and the day of vengeance of our God, / to comfort all who mourn." For a last example, Paul exhorts, "Beloved, never avenge yourselves, but leave room for the wrath of God, for it is written, 'Vengeance is mine, I will repay, says the Lord'" (Romans 12:19). Paul is referring to Deuteronomy 32:35a. For some who mourn the victims of murder, the execution of the perpetrator provides comfort; others find no comfort in another life being taken. Some find comfort in the image that the perpetrator will suffer in the afterlife; some do not.

Abel's "bloods," his posterity, cried out from the ground, and so Genesis asks us to look at the next generations. While Cain and, especially, Lamech are remembered for destruction, their children are remembered for creation. Lamech and Adah's children include Jabal, "the ancestor of those who live in tents and have livestock" (4:20). The child reminds me of Abel. Their son Jubal is "the ancestor of all those who play the lyre and pipe" (4:21), both men and women, with music used to stir us to battle or to soothe the soul. Lamech and Zillah's children include Tubal-cain, "who made all kinds of bronze and iron tools" (4:22). Again, we can raise the question of what these products are for—jewelry and plows or weapons and chariots? The permutations of the *J-B-L* root (or, better, since Hebrew does not have a "J," the letters *Y-B-L*), which we detect in these names, also give us the term "Jubilee" (see Leviticus 25:10) or, in Hebrew, *yovel.*

"The sister of Tubal-cain was Na'amah" (4:22): Her story is lost to us. Her name means "pleasant." King Solomon had a wife, named Na'amah, an Ammonite. She was the mother of Rehoboam, the next king, whose vanity and immaturity prompted the secession of the ten northern tribes (1 Kings 14:21). These women have their own stories, and we may want to fill in the gaps. They allow us to imagine being the daughter of a murderer, the sister of artisans, a foreign wife in King Solomon's harem, the foreign mother of the heir to Israel's throne.

The Third Son

For the first time since the expulsion from the garden, the narrator returns to the first couple. "Adam knew his wife again, and she bore a son and named him Seth [Hebrew for "put, appoint"], for she said, 'God has appointed for me another child (Hebrew *zerah*, "seed") instead of Abel, because Cain killed him" (4:25). Nothing about how Adam and Eve reacted to Abel's murder or even if they buried his body. Nothing about their feelings toward Cain or his toward them. Eve had "gotten" (*qanah*) Cain with God's help, and with God's help, Cain will not be killed, but there is no sense that she will see her firstborn again. Now God has "appointed" for her another son, but Seth cannot replace Cain, any more than one child, or spouse, can replace another.

I'm also intrigued by the use of the term "seed" in Eve's response. In 4:1, Eve stated, "I have produced (Hebrew *qanah*, "gotten") a man (*ish*) with the help of the Lord." Now she has a "seed." "Man" suggested to me a full-grown, mature individual. "Seed" suggests potential. Perhaps Eve has learned something about the need for caring and guiding parents. The term "seed" also sends us back to 3:15, where God tells the snake, "I will put enmity between you and the woman/ and between your offspring [lit: "your seed"] and hers [lit: "her seed"]." This seed, this new child, will require both instruction from parents and protection from natural enemies.

Eve may recall, in watching Seth grow up, Cain and Abel as infants and as toddlers. She may regret what she failed to do, or she may find feelings of love evoked as good memories arise. Seth cannot replace her first two children, but he can remind her of them. One hopes the memories are of comfort.

"To Seth also a son was born, and he named him Enosh. At that time people began to invoke the name of the LORD" (4:26). With all the naming of the antediluvian figures, now there is a concern for the name of the divine. While parents name children, and the first man names his wife *Chava* (the Hebrew form of Eve), and while people do invoke God's name, as Eve did upon naming Cain, no one yet bestows a name on God. The first person to do this is Hagar, the wife of Abraham and mother of Ishmael (16:13).

Despite the difficulties of this chapter, replete with jealousy, murder, alienation, celebration of vengeance, the invoking of God seems to be the right step. Two steps backward, out of Eden, east of Eden, and now perhaps a step forward. Psalm 133:1 exults, "How very good and pleasant it is / when kindred live together in unity!" The Hebrew underlying "pleasant" is the same word as the name "Na'amah," Lamech's daughter. The Hebrew is better translated, "Behold, how good and pleasant it is when brothers [and sisters] sit [or dwell] together as one [or in unity]." "Kindred" fails to find a connection to the "brothers" Cain and Abel. Psalm 133 is a beacon or a goal. Genesis 4 is a story of what can happen; it is not a mandate for what must happen.

CHAPTER 3

Noah

Noah is the poster child for the overcommitted. When we think of ourselves as drowning in paperwork, up to our eyeballs in emails, treading water at the job, when we want to jump ship or recognize the project is dead in the water, we can imagine Noah. His task seems impossible: not only building an ark but managing all the birds, animals, creepy crawlies, a wife, three sons and their wives. Compared to Noah, things don't seem so bad.

Noah also presents a moral conundrum. Did he warn his fellow humans, or did he build the boat only to save himself and his family? Did he care about the people and the animals who died, or was he concerned only that he and his family survived? Did he feel survivor's guilt, or did he think that he deserved the grace he was shown? Was his planting a vineyard a benefit to humanity or another food that creates a curse? How do we understand his cursing of his grandson?

Not only are Noah's actions morally problematic, but so are God's. Is a universal flood a good idea, especially since it did not work to wipe out evil? Humanity remains inclined to evil. What is the best response to a natural disaster? Do we want a God only of mercy, or do we want justice as well? Is universal destruction to be celebrated, mourned, or prevented if possible?

We enter these waters slowly and carefully.

Origins of Our Stories

The story of Noah reflects communal memories of floods and the attendant devastation and death. Catastrophes have been part of life since life began. Whether the meteor that wiped out the dinosaurs (with the exceptions of the *Flintstones*' Dino, Barney, or the Sinclairs [points to you if you remember them]), earthquakes, volcanic eruptions, fires and freezes, locusts and red tide, or plagues and pandemics, or, yes, floods, there is instability to earthly existence. Disasters can create trauma. They can also prompt resilience. The drive to persevere rather than to give up is part of what makes us humans.

We also want explanations for such catastrophes. While science can explain meteors and shifting of tectonic plates and locust swarms and diseases, we frequently look for nonnatural or supernatural explanations: the disaster must have been caused by our own misdeeds or we are being tested or we are paying the penalty for the sins of generations past or we have allowed groups who do not look like us or worship like us to continue to exist and so we seek a scapegoat. At times, as with Noah's flood, the Bible explains the cause; at other times, it does not.

Stories of a universal flood or of the famine that brings Abraham and then Jacob and his sons to Egypt or of the ten plagues God inflicts in Egypt because of the population's willingness to enslave the Israelites and then kill their newborn sons are not simply memories of memories or records of history. The narrator did not need to preserve such tales. Rather, they are designed to challenge us, to prepare us for the worst that can happen, to help us see that our actions can have repercussions for our children and our children's children. They ask about resilience and resistance, about justice and mercy, about the responsibilities of survivors and the memories of the dead.

The events they record happened long, long ago and far, far away. They happened once upon a time; they happened before writing was invented and so were passed along, generation to generation, like a game of telephone tag, where storytellers embellished given the interests of their audiences. Eventually, these stories were written down by people in different times and locations, in Assyria and Babylon and ancient Israel. They contain similar motifs—how evil entered the world, divine responses, a flood that wiped out everyone and everything, save for some lucky individuals. But because they are timeless, we can locate ourselves in them, consider what they mean, learn from them, and be challenged by them. Such is the case with Genesis 6–9, the story of Noah and the ark.

Noah in Historical Context

The story of Noah is not the only flood narrative. The region of Sumer, established in the sixth millennium BCE between the Tigris and Euphrates River (on today's map, Iraq), gives us the city of Ur, the original home of the patriarch Abraham (11:28), cuneiform writing, and a flood story featuring the hero Zuisudra (his name means "life of long days"). The cuneiform text recording his story dates to ca. 1600 BCE.

From the Epic of Gilgamesh comes the story of Utnapishtim ("he who has found life"), a human ordered by the god Enki to leave his earthly concerns and build a boat, called "Preserver of Life" (I prefer "Life Preserver" or even "Life Saver") to survive a forthcoming flood. The most complete text of the Gilgamesh epic is preserved on clay tablets from the library of King Ashurbanipal of Assyria (ruled 669–631 BCE following the tenure of his father, Esar-haddon; for biblical connections, see 2 Kings 19:37). Both Old Babylonian and Neo-Assyrian cuneiform texts dating ca. 1700 BCE record the Atrahasis epic: same story, different hero. Berossus, a Babylonian historian writing ca. 290 BCE notes a flood in his *Babylonaika*. His work, preserved in fragments, was used by both the first-century Jewish historian Josephus and the fourth-century Christian historian Eusebius. Extrabiblical accounts that resemble scriptural narratives did not discombobulate them, and they should not discombobulate us either.

Finally, the first-century CE Latin poet Ovid tells of Philemon and Baucis, an elderly couple from Phrygia who show hospitality to Zeus and Hermes. The gods were traveling incognito, and they sought in vain to find lodging: we can hear echoes of the story of Sodom and Gomorrah in Genesis 19: cities destroyed because they "had pride, excess of food, and prosperous ease but did not aid the poor and needy" (Ezekiel 16:49). We can also find a connection to Acts 14:12 where in Lystra, the locals mistake Barnabas and Paul for, respectively, Zeus and Hermes (they equate Paul with Hermes because he is the chief speaker).

At their dinner with the gods, Baucis notes that the pitcher of wine was never empty. This motif appears in multiple sources, including 1 Kings 17:16, where the prophet Elijah receives hospitality from the widow of Zarephath: "The jar of meal was not emptied, neither did the jug of oil fail." Zeus then tells Philemon and Baucis to leave their home, climb a mountain, and not turn back until reaching the summit (we might "remember Lot's wife" [Luke 17:32] who turned back to look at her home in Sodom and was turned into a pillar of salt [Genesis 19:26]). When the couple finally looks, they see that a flood has destroyed their town. In the aftermath of the flood, the gods turn their modest home into a temple, Baucis and Philemon become the local priests, and when they die, a metamorphosis takes place: they become trees whose branches intertwine.

Lessons of divine benevolence and divine response to evil, justice and vengeance, righteousness and passivity, the role of survivors, the importance of nature, starting over and reflecting back: each story gives rise to new questions.

Genealogies

Genesis 5:1-32, one of those long genealogies most readers are inclined to skip over, resembles 4:18-26, the genealogy where we meet Lamech and his wives (see the previous chapter). Some people trace their ancestry to the Norman conquest, to the pilgrims who landed on Plymouth Rock, to towns in Poland or Italy, Senegal or Gambia. Others discover family members by genetic testing or internet sleuthing. And sometimes we get different versions of the same family story. This second genealogy in Genesis 5 looks like spin control to me: it ensures that Noah and therefore all humanity descend not from Cain but from Seth.

It also redeems Lamech—at least partially. This second genealogy says nothing about the wives or about the revenge. Rather, it tells us that Lamech died at the age of 777 (5:31). This seems like a revision of the earlier references to seven and seven-times-seven retribution. Further, Genesis 5:28-29 states, "When Lamech had lived one hundred eighty-two years, he became the father of a son; he named him Noah [Hebrew for "comfort" and also connoting "relief"], saying, 'Out of the ground that the Lord has cursed this one shall bring us relief from our work and from the toil of our hands.'" That Noah is the first person born after Adam's death suggests a new start—that although God had cursed the ground, the ground now becomes the source of comfort: the curse can be countered. The verbal form of the name "Noah" appears multiple times in the Bible; my favorite is Isaiah 40:1, where God exhorts (in the plural, not only to Isaiah himself but also to the heavenly council and anyone else listening), "Comfort, O comfort my people" (Hebrew: *nachamu nachamu ammi*). Their exile is ending, and they are to be repatriated to their homeland. Land, here the sense of homeland, can also provide comfort. Finally, speaking of "comfort," one translation of the Greek term *paraclete*, the word John's Gospel (e.g., John 14:26 KJV) uses for the Holy Spirit, is "comforter."

Genesis 6 gives us generational options: Cain or Seth, murderers or artisans, vengeance or comfort, calling on the divine or promoting the self. It also prompts us to wonder how things got so bad that God sent a flood to wipe out all but Noah and the others with him on the ark.

A New Problem and a New Origin for Evil

Genesis 6:1-7 is a tantalizing hint of what may have been a much more developed account; it offers an alternative to the story of Adam and Eve and the expulsion from Eden in Genesis 3. "When people began to multiply on the face of the ground, and daughters were born to them, the sons of God [Hebrew: *b'nai Elohim*] saw that they were fair, and they took wives for themselves of all that they chose" (6:1-2). The text mentions daughters: no notice of "sons" or "brothers"; no mention of parental involvement; no mention that the women had a choice in their fate. They were "taken." The text recollects Greek myths of gods impregnating women: such relations result in demigods such as Hercules, Theseus, and Perseus, and, according to ancient propaganda, Alexander the Great and Augustus Caesar. There is nothing in any of these stories of an angel gaining Mary's consent for her miraculous pregnancy (Luke 1:38).

These *b'nai Elohim*, "sons of God," reappear in Job 1:6 and 2:1 (the NRSVue offers "heavenly beings") as members of the divine court. They are the "us" in Genesis 1:26, where God says, "Let us make humans in our image, according to our likeness." One of them, at least according to Job, is "the satan" (a title, the "adversary"; not "Satan," the divine opponent).

Eve and, with her, Adam wanted to be like the gods. They gained the knowledge of good and evil and so maturity, for to be like the gods is to lack childhood innocence and to be aware of the consequences of one's actions. But God exiled Adam and Eve from Eden before they could eat from the tree of life and live forever. Genesis 6 hints at another opportunity to be like the gods: via divine parentage. God starts a correction to this goal by limiting the human lifespan to 120 years (6:3). By the way, Deuteronomy 34:7 states, "Moses was one hundred twenty years old when he died; his sight was unimpaired, and his vigor had not abated." Good for him!

Limiting the human lifespan does not prevent this impulse to gain divinity. The next verse, Genesis 6:4, notes, "The Nephilim were on the earth in those days—and also afterward—when the sons of God went in to the daughters of humans, who bore children to them. These were the heroes that were of old, warriors of renown." The translation "heroes" is generous. The Hebrew *geborim* means "mighty men" or "strong men," and not all strong men are "heroes." For Jephthah, the judge who sacrifices his daughter, the NRSVue translates the same term (*gibor*) as "warrior" (Judges 11:1).

The term *Nephilim* comes from the Hebrew root *N-Ph-L*, which means "to fall." Thus, Genesis 6:4 serves as one origin for stories of fallen angels. For example, 2 Peter 2:4-5 reads, "For if God did not *spare the angels when they sinned* but cast them into hell and committed them to chains of deepest darkness to be kept until the judgment; and if he did not spare the ancient world, even though he saved Noah, a herald of righteousness, with seven others, when he brought a flood on the world of the ungodly. . . . " (emphasis added). Again, the Bible is concerned that humans not seek to be gods: that quest gives us too much power. As the English philosopher Lord Acton said, "Power corrupts, and absolute power corrupts absolutely." The Septuagint describes the

Nephilim as "giants," and hence the KJV translation as well as the title of the O. E. Rolvaag novel, *Giants in the Earth,* which I remember reading in high school.

According to Genesis 6:5, God saw that the " wickedness of humans was great in the earth and that every inclination of the thoughts of their hearts was only evil continually." While the Bible does not explicitly state that this evil was caused by the mixing of divine and human, the narrative context hints at it. For Genesis 6, evil is superhuman in origin. The earth's problem was not the fruit in the garden; it was the move on the part of heavenly beings to reproduce with human women. The evil this new generation concocts makes Cain's fratricide and Lamech's revenge look like walks in the park.

We can attribute acts of both supererogation (a great word) and infamy to supernatural—divine or satanic—power. I'm inclined to see both extremes, of great good and great evil, as human products. To state that great good requires supernatural help can diminish human potential or suggest that only some people have such gifts. To state that the great evil is demonically sourced gives perpetrators too much power, even as it threatens to remove responsibility from them (as in the case of those who claim, "The devil made me do it").

Moreover, once we associate people with a genetic predisposition to evil—once we see them as children of the "fallen ones"—it becomes easier both to avoid challenging them and to demonize them. According to Numbers 13:31-33, the Israelite scouts Moses sent into Canaan remark on the inhabitants: "We are not able to go up against this people, for they are stronger than we.... All the people that we saw in [the land] are of great size. There we saw the Nephilim... and to ourselves we seemed like grasshoppers, and so we seemed to them." The enemy is superhuman and a threat: such is the role of propaganda in that it dehumanizes the enemy. They may look heroic, but we know how they got that way: they are not like us; they are unnatural; they must be destroyed.

Genesis 6:6-7 turns to God, here by no means an immovable, distant creator. "The LORD was sorry that he had made humans on the earth, and it grieved him to his heart." I appreciate this comment. God blames himself for the problem. God made humanity; God gave us free will; God allowed us to do what we wanted. And the result was evil. I hear echoes of the man's comment, "The woman whom you gave to be with me" (3:12).

The human heart is inclined toward wickedness; the divine heart is inclined toward grief at this wickedness. Connections between God and humanity run even more deeply. The Hebrew term translated "grieve," *etzev*, is the same term we heard in Genesis 3, "I will make your *etzev* (NRSVue "pangs") in childbirth exceedingly great; / in *etzev* (NRSVue "pain"), you shall bring forth children" (3:16). The pain/toil/grief the woman experiences now God experiences. Yet, it is this pain/toil/grief that Noah will relieve, "Out of the ground that the LORD has cursed this one shall bring us relief from our work and from the *etzev* (NRSVue "toil") of our hands" (5:29). We grieve, as does God. The grief can be redressed; the question is how.

"So the LORD said, 'I will blot out from the earth the humans I have created—people together with animals and creeping things and birds of the air—for I am sorry that I have made them'" (6:7). When my children were little, they asked about this story. What about little children? What did the animals do wrong? Why would God want to drown puppies and kittens? These are good questions, and I'm glad the children asked. We talked about how this is a story people told a very long time ago, and we don't have the opportunity to ask them what they had in mind. But we could guess. The children offered several answers: Maybe dogs and cats were nasty back then, and they bit little kids or pooped in the house. Maybe we are nicer today than people were back then. Maybe God just wanted a do-over. When they told me they still felt sorry for all the people and animals, even if they had done bad things, I encouraged those responses. We talked about what happens if we hurt someone else, why people sometimes hurt other people or take their toys or call them names, what they would do if they saw others being naughty, and other such situations. You may think of your own questions and responses.

Humanity got a do-over with the genealogy of Seth replacing that of Cain, with the change in the picture of Lamech from one of vengeance to one of comfort. Now God gets a do-over. Creation will be uncreated. As the world was created with the separation of the waters above from the waters below and the emergence of dry land, so now the floods will destroy everything.

The do-over motif appears elsewhere in the Bible. Isaiah 11:6-9d describes the peaceable kingdom where "the wolf shall live with the lamb" (and the lamb will not be nervous); Isaiah 65:17 repeats the vision while speaking of "new heavens and a new earth"; 2 Peter 3:13 similarly awaits "new heavens and a new earth" (also see Revelation 21:1). Each generation hopes for the redemption and thinks it is near, and each generation continues to wait.

We can respond to the notice that "every inclination of the thoughts of their hearts was only evil" (Genesis 6:5). The rabbis, reflecting on the notion of free will, concluded that human beings have both an "evil inclination" (Hebrew: *yetzer ha-ra'*) and a "good inclination" (Hebrew: *yetzer ha-tov*). The evil inclination gives rise to selfishness and to the competitive spirit. *Genesis Rabbah* 9.7, reflecting patriarchal language, observes, "Without the evil inclination, no man would build a house, take a wife and beget children; and so said Solomon, 'Then I saw that all toil and all skill in work come from one person's envy of another.

This also is vanity and a chasing after wind'" [from Ecclesiastes 4:4]. We can tame this evil inclination and harness it for the good. To build a home, to create a family, to work hard, even to compete as a means of stretching ourselves, are all virtues.

Pirke Avot 1:14 quotes Rabbi Hillel, who lived about half a century before Jesus, as saying, "If I am not for myself, who will be for me?" The inability to recognize our own good contribution to society or to take pride in our work can give rise to feelings of worthlessness or resentment. But to be for ourselves also requires selfishness, pride, competition, and the desire for victory. It requires the evil inclination. Hillel continues, "If I am for myself alone, what am I?" We cannot only promote ourselves: we are related to everyone else and even to the earth. Without the evil inclination, we would be swallowed up. Without the good inclination, we would swallow up everything. The challenge is to find a balance.

Noah and the Ark

Genesis 6:8 states,"Noah found favor in the sight of the LORD," and 6:9 adds, "Noah was a righteous man, blameless in his generation; Noah walked with God." He is comparable to his ancestor Enoch, who also "walked with God" (5:22, 24). Indeed, he is the first person identified in the Bible as "righteous" (Hebrew *tzaddiq*; Greek *dikaios*), and he is in the company of other people the Bible calls "righteous," people who do what is right. Judah describes his daughter-in-law Tamar, whom he took to be a prostitute and impregnated her, as "more righteous than I" (38:26 [the NRSVue gives the anemic "she is more in the right than I"]). Tamar, the first woman mentioned in the New Testament (see Matthew 1:3), risks not only her reputation but also her life to further her goals. In 1 Samuel 24:17, King Saul says to David, "You are more righteous than I, for you have repaid me good, whereas I have repaid you evil." David also risks his life in his run for the throne. King Solomon describes "Abner son of Ner, commander of the army of Israel, and Amasa son of Jether, commander of the army of Judah" as more righteous than Joab, the commander of David's army (1 Kings 2:32).

Matthew 1:19 identifies Joseph as a "righteous man" who was unwilling to make a scandal of Mary's unexpected pregnancy. Mark 6:20 notes that Herod Antipas viewed John the Baptizer as a "righteous and holy man." Luke identifies as righteous the Baptizer's parents, Elizabeth and Zechariah (1:6), the elderly Simeon who encounters the baby Jesus with Mary and Joseph in the Jerusalem Temple (2:25), and Joseph of Arimathea (23:50). According to Acts 10:22, the centurion Cornelius is "righteous." The hospitable sheep in the famous parable of the sheep and the goats (Matthew 25:37) are righteous. These texts ask us to study these figures to determine what constitutes "righteousness." Do we consider ourselves righteous? If so, based on what? Do we consider our heroes—politicians, movie stars, athletes—as righteous? If we could choose one word by which we would be remembered, would it be "righteous"?

Finally, Jesus is "righteous," although some translations mask the identification. According to Matthew 27:19, Mrs. Pilate sends word to her husband, who is interrogating Jesus, "Have nothing to do with that innocent man, for today I have suffered a great deal because of a dream about him." Behind the term "innocent" is the Greek *dikaios*, "righteous." Similarly, according to Luke 23:47, at the cross, "When the centurion saw what had taken place, he praised God and said, 'Certainly this man was innocent.'" Again, behind "innocent" is *dikaios*, "righteous."

Noting the qualification "in his generation," the Babylonian Talmud (*b. Sanhedrin* 108a) describes Noah as comparable to a jar of wine stored in a cellar amid jars of vinegar. While the fragrance of the wine might otherwise go undetected, amid the jars of vinegar, it is noted. In other words, I wouldn't date Noah. I've tried to like him. I recognize that Ezekiel 14:14 compares him to Job and Daniel, two other Gentiles who saved others and not just themselves. I've seen the children's books in which Noah resembles Santa Claus (minus the red suit) and plays with bunnies. There's also my friend Sandy Sasso's book about Mrs. Noah, who saved the plants (I have more sympathy for Mrs. Noah, about whom the Bible says nothing. If Zillah and Ada can get a few mentions, one might think Mrs. Noah would appear. Here's another story left for us to tell).

Genesis 6:9-10 surrounds the notice of Noah's righteousness with familial details: "These are the descendants of Noah. . . . Noah had three sons: Shem, Ham, and Japheth." We also learn from this verse that not only the sons, but also grandchildren and great-grandchildren will continue in Noah's line. While the NRSVue mentions "descendants" the Hebrew, *toldot*, means "generations."

Genesis 6:11-12 repeats, two times more, how God *saw* the corruption. The problem is not simply evil thoughts; it metastasizes into evil action. Hebrew has, compared to English, a much more limited vocabulary, and when words repeat, ancient audiences attuned to oral storytelling paid attention. The Hebrew term for corruption or destruction is *shakhat* (that *kh* is a guttural, as in Bach); it is the same term Genesis 6:13 uses to describe the flood's destruction. Perhaps we do better to read, "God saw the *destruction*" humans made and so finished what we had started. Corruption leads to destruction. The term is also used in Exodus 32:7, the incident with the golden calf (the NRSVue offers "acted perversely"—the golden calf was not one of ancient Israel's better moments) and in Isaiah 11:9, when "they will not hurt or *shachat* [destroy/corrupt] / on all my holy mountain, / for the earth will be full of the knowledge of the LORD, / as the waters cover the sea." Finally, on language, Genesis 6:11 states both that the earth was "corrupt" (*shachat*) and that it was "filled with violence." Coincidentally, the Hebrew behind "violence" is *chamas*, which sounds like the Arabic *hamas*, meaning "zeal" (it is also an acronym for Harakat al-Muqawama al-Islamiya, the Islamic Resistance Movement. One group's violence is another's zeal; one group's patriot is another's terrorist. It helps, again, to remember that we are all in the divine image; we are all related. I know this sounds pie-in-the-sky, idealistic and simplistic; I also know that it is true.

Noah lives amid this corrupt, or destructive, generation, and he "walked with God," but such walking is not enough. Noah reminds me of mystics across all traditions who prioritize personal spirituality over relationships with others. I wonder what Noah *did* to demonstrate his righteousness.

God tells Noah, "I have determined to make an end of all flesh, for the earth is filled with violence because of them [this is God's fifth notice]; now I am going to destroy them along with the earth [sixth notice]" (6:13). Noah had numerous opportunities to raise a question. When God tells Abraham that he is going to destroy Sodom and Gomorrah, Abraham recoils: "Far be it from you to do such a thing, to slay the righteous with the wicked, so that the righteous fare as the wicked! Far be that from you! Shall not the Judge of all the earth do what is just?" (18:25). Ten righteous people would have saved the cities.

Noah could have said something. Or perhaps no righteous were present.

Destruction could have been instantaneous—a meteor or an earthquake. God could have boomed down a voice from heaven. God could have commissioned Noah to preach to the locals, as Jonah (another near-drowning victim!) preached to the Ninevites. But no, God simply tells Noah, "Make yourself an ark of cypress wood" three hundred cubits long, fifty cubits wide, thirty cubits high, with three decks, and the roof a cubit above to allow for light (6:14-16). A cubit is 18 inches, so the ark measures 450 × 75 × 45 feet. By the way, the ark has no rudder: it will land where it will land. This also saves Noah any worry about navigating.

The Hebrew term for ark, *tevah*, appears only one other time in the Bible: Exodus 2:3 states regarding Moses's mother, "When she could hide him no longer she got a papyrus *tevah* (NRSVue "basket") for him and plastered it with bitumen and pitch; she put the child in it and placed it among the reeds on the bank of the river." This story also has connections to the Tower of Babel. The wickedness God saw at the time of Noah is replicated by the wickedness of the Egyptians, who obeyed Pharaoh by drowning Hebrew baby boys in the Nile. The plagues then replicate the flood. And one woman, Moses's mother, acts like Noah to protect her son. She builds an ark not because God commands; she acts on her own initiative because her heart was not inclined toward evil. And that one act made all the difference for the Israelites.

Back to Noah's story, where God lowers the boom (I'm trying to avoid nautical puns; sometimes I go overboard): "I am going to bring a flood of waters on the earth, to destroy from under heaven all flesh in which is the breath of life; everything that is on the earth shall die" (6:17). We've heard this before, a lot.

Still no word from Noah. It would take a while for construction—plenty of time for Noah to question the wisdom of the flood or tell his neighbors about why he is building an ark (I suspect they would have asked). Rabbinic tradition suggests that the construction started with Noah's planting the seed for the cypress trees, which gives even more time for the possibility of witnessing. Did they think Noah was three sheets to the wind (I'm sorry)?

In Matthew 24:37-39 (also see Luke 17:26-27), Jesus states, "As the days of Noah were, so will be the coming of the Son of Man. For as in the days before the flood they were eating and drinking, marrying and giving in marriage, until the day when Noah entered the ark, and they knew nothing until the flood came and swept them all away, so, too, will be the coming of the Son of Man." In this interpretation, the people had no clue about the flood. Jesus here seems to anticipate another flood, and so sees his current generation, the generation of the Roman Empire, as comparable to that ancient time. We may wonder: How bad can things get? Is universal destruction the answer? Might there be a better answer?

Hebrews 11:7 affirms, "By faith Noah, warned by God about events as yet unseen, respected the warning and built an ark to save his household; by this he condemned the world and became an heir to the righteousness that is in accordance with faith." The building is the condemnation—nothing here about prophetic critique or neighborly concern. When destruction comes, do we save only our own in a bomb shelter or a mountaintop hideaway or do we seek to love our neighbors as ourselves?

Such questions also remind me of Matthew 2, where Joseph, another righteous man, is warned in a dream to take baby Jesus and Mary and flee to Egypt to escape Herod's soldiers. He warned no one, and so the soldiers slaughter the babies and toddlers in Bethlehem. When do we save ourselves, and when do we save others? Is our responsibility first to our family, or should it be universal? These are questions that surface in today's politics, but they are as old as the flood narratives. The stories tell us that we can never do enough and at the same time ask us what we can do. One righteous person can save a city or a world.

Next comes the Bible's first covenant, made with Noah and extending to his wife, his sons, and their wives (6:18). The Bible does not tell us whether the wife, sons, and daughters-in-law are with Noah when this covenant is made. Nor does it recount what they thought about Noah's relationship to God. Were my husband one day to announce, "I'm building a boat, and we need to get the children and their dogs on board," I'd be very worried about what he had been watching on the internet.

God gives Noah the details. According to Genesis 6:19, he is to bring two of "every living thing, of all flesh . . . into the ark . . . they shall be male and female." However, according to Genesis 7:2, he is to take "seven pairs of all clean animals, the male and its mate; and a pair of the animals that are not clean, the male and its mate." How Noah knew clean from unclean is unclear: the dietary regulations will not be detailed until the time of Moses. Source-critics, whom we met in chapter 1 concerning the distinctions between the two Creation narratives, suggest that there are two (or more) hands behind the texts, with the priestly writers (as in Genesis 1) offering the seven-by-seven and the J source, the twosies by twosies (alumni of summer camps will catch this reference). Could be. The seven-by-seven is more practical here: Noah will eventually offer an animal sacrifice, and the two-by-two model would then mean the extinction of certain species.

Noah does what God commands. We don't know how Noah sexed the rabbits, caught the cheetahs, or separated the elephants from the herds.

The Flood

Genesis 7 begins with (yet another) repetition of the world's wickedness and Noah's righteousness. God orders Noah and the family into the ark because "I have seen that you alone are righteous before me in this generation" (7:1). I can picture Mrs. Noah wondering what God thinks of her.

The flood is the undoing of creation. "In the six hundredth year of Noah's life, in the second month, on the seventeenth day of the month, on that day all the fountains of the great deep burst forth, and the windows of the heavens were opened. The rain fell on the earth forty days and forty nights" (7:11-12). Genesis 1 describes the separation of the waters above and the waters below to create dry land. Now the waters are released from their heavenly and subterranean borders. But there is also a difference. The separation in Genesis 1 prepared the way for life. While Noah and his family and some of the animals are safe on the ark (7:13), now there is death, lots of death.

"And all flesh died that moved on the earth, birds, domestic animals, wild animals, all swarming creatures that swarm on the earth, and all human beings; everything on dry land in whose nostrils was the breath of life (Hebrew *nishmat ruach chayyim*: "breath of the spirit of life") died" (7:21-22). These are not details lightly to be passed over. The narrator gives us the details and so asks us to think about them. Yet I suspect many of us do skip over these details, just as we have become immune to the disasters that we watch on television and internet feeds. If we slow down and read the details the Bible gives us, perhaps we will learn to slow down and take in fully what we see in our own lives.

Then the refrain: "Only Noah was left and those with him in the ark" (7:23). I wonder what Noah and his family were thinking: thank God we're alive, those poor creatures, the ark smells, I miss my home, what will happen to us now, watch out for the dung. I try not to think of disasters, let alone consider what I would do were I in one. But I do know that the one thing I would do if disaster struck is tell my family and friends that I love them. Having smoke alarms, fire extinguishers, and an emergency medical kit is also helpful.

Some later traditions understand the flood metaphorically. For example, 1 Peter 3:20-21 regards the flood waters, which clean out human wickedness, as a type of baptism: "When God waited patiently in the days of Noah, during the building of the ark, in which a few, that is, eight lives, were saved through water. And baptism, which this prefigured, now saves you—not as a removal of dirt from the body but as an appeal to God for a good conscience, through the resurrection of Jesus Christ." I know adults who, upon being baptized, felt a sense not only emotionally but also in their bodies that they are entering new life. Death to sin is one thing; the death of sinners is something else.

After the Flood

Genesis 8:1 begins, "But God remembered Noah" and all the animals, and this memory prompts God to send a wind to remove the waters. Had there been no ark, there would be nothing and no one to remember. The Hebrew text stresses the importance of memory. The Hebrew term is *zachar*, the root of the name Zechariah ("the Lord remembers"), the father of John the Baptizer. The Jewish memorial service is called *yizkor*, meaning "may [God] remember"; its prayers include *El male rachamin* ("God, full of mercy") and *Av Ha-rachamim* ("Father of mercies"). We say these prayers to remember our loved ones; we say them for people who have no family to recite them. We are not immortal, but we can memorialize the names. We can remember our loved ones, our friends, the people in our communities. Ideally, we will remember them as righteous.

The theme of memory recurs in the next chapter, where God tells Noah, "I will remember my covenant that is between me and you and every living creature of all flesh, and the waters shall never again become a flood to destroy all flesh. When the bow is in the clouds, I will see it and remember the everlasting covenant between God and every living creature of all flesh that is on the earth" (9:15-16). The same motif recurs in 19:29, "when God destroyed the cities of the plain [Sodom and Gomorrah], God remembered Abraham and sent Lot out of the midst of the overthrow, when he overthrew the cities in which Lot had settled." In 30:22, "God remembered Rachel, and God heeded her and opened her womb"; in Exodus 2:24, God hears the groaning of the enslaved Israelites, "and God remembered his covenant with Abraham, Isaac, and Jacob." The settings concern danger and desperation. At times when we fear no one remembers us and no one cares, the Bible insists that God remembers.

Echoes in the text are also prompts to memory. For example, Genesis 8:1 states, "God made a wind blow over the earth, and the waters subsided." The Hebrew for wind, *ruach* (another guttural, like Bach), can also mean "breath" or "spirit." We heard the term in Genesis 1:2, where "the mighty wind" or "the spirit of God" (both translations fit the Hebrew *ruach elohim*) sweeps over the face of the earth. In 7:22, every "breath (of the spirit, *ruach*) of life died." With this wind, a new creation is about to happen.

The waters abate, "and in the seventh month, on the seventeenth day of the month, the ark came to rest on the mountains of Ararat" (8:4). Mountains, plural. So much for all those books and shows about finding Noah's ark on Mount Ararat. Nor has the ark been found. I doubt it will be; I also note that few are interested in finding the arks of other ancient flood stories. We do not need to believe in the facticity of Noah's ark to find meaning in a story of universal wickedness, singular righteousness, humanity's relation to nature, issues of survival, and many other ideas the story presents.

After forty days, Noah opens the ark's window. Forty days, or forty anything, suggests a fullness: Isaac was forty when he married Rebecca; forty years of wilderness wandering; Jesus spent forty days in the wilderness; today, many of us spend forty years in the workforce and then retire. I think back forty years—the time my first child was born, the year of my first job—it's an interesting exercise, a prompt to memory, a generation ago.

Noah sends out a raven; the text does not tell us why a raven. Ravens are more or less indistinguishable from crows (I looked this up); they are noisy scavengers that eat carrion. Collective terms for ravens include conspiracy, treachery, rave, and unkindness. Better the pride of lions and the parliament of owls. Perhaps Noah thought the bird was clever; perhaps he was glad to have an excuse to get it out of the ark.

The raven does not come back; instead, it flies back and forth until the waters dry up. No doubt that raven has a story to tell. I also wonder what the raven's mate, still on the ark, was thinking. Perhaps the raven is the indicator that not everything on the new earth will be calm and peaceful. Animals will die, and the raven will scavenge.

We don't know how long after the raven left that Noah sent the next bird, a dove. The dove, which is more or less the same thing as a pigeon (I looked this up, too), is known for calmness and mournful cooing. The collectives include bevy, cote, and piteousness. In this case, the dove, unable to find a place to land, returns to the ark.

Seven days later, Noah tries again. This time, the dove returns with an olive leaf in its beak. Horticulture is not my strong suit (it's up there with gardening), but I doubt that an olive tree, submerged for forty days or more, would be in great shape. Then again, strange things happen in the Bible. Noah waits another seven days, sends out the dove again, and this time it does not return.

"In the six hundred first year, in the first month, on the first day of the month, the waters were dried up from the earth, and Noah removed the covering of the ark and looked and saw that the face of the ground was drying" (8:13). The first day of the first month would not be January 1. In ancient Mesopotamia, the date would have been in the spring. On the Hebrew calendar, the first day of the first month is the first day of Nissan, and the fourteenth of Nissan is the first night of the Passover holiday. The next time the Bible mentions the first day of the first month is in Exodus 40:2 (cf. 40:17) in the commandment to set up the wilderness tabernacle (or "tent of meeting"). Thus, the worship system is connected with this do-over. As Noah is a new Adam (and Mrs. Noah, a new Eve), so anyone who worships becomes a new creation, responsible for choosing the good and rejecting the bad.

One month and twenty-seven days later, the earth is dry. Time to leave. But Noah does not move on his own. The raven left; the dove left. Noah waits for permission to leave. God tells him to disembark along with his sons and their wives and the birds and animals. Noah is not the model of personal initiative.

Finally, Noah acts on his own. He builds an altar and offers pure animals and birds (good thing he had pairs of seven; the pigs and bunnies were much relieved). We might remember the earlier sacrifice, that of Cain (vegetables) and Abel (sheep); the sacrifices there did not end well. There is a sacrifice; there are brothers—there's going to be a catch.

> *When the* L*ORD smelled the pleasing odor, the* L*ORD said in his heart, "I will never again curse the ground because of humans, for the inclination of the human heart is evil from youth; nor will I ever again destroy every living creature as I have done.*
>
> *As long as the earth endures,*
> *seedtime and harvest, cold and heat,*
> *summer and winter,*
> *day and night shall not cease."*
>
> (*Genesis 8:21-22*)

The sacrifice is not seen, not heard, not tasted or touched, but smelled. According to the Epic of Gilgamesh, when Utna-pishtim offered a sacrifice after surviving the flood, the gods smelled the sweet savor and gathered "like flies" at the altar. That's not a great image.

While the ancients did not have the scientific knowledge of olfaction, they likely knew that mothers and babies can identify each other by smell. The sense of smell impacts us viscerally. When a person leaves the room, we lose sight and sound, touch and (depending on how close we are) taste. But a scent lingers. The smell of a certain perfume can remind us not only of the person wearing it but also of where we were and what we were doing when we first smelled it. Our eyes might lead us to think a food is tasty, but our sense of smell will keep us from consuming what is spoiled. For me, the particular smell that old libraries or bookstores have makes me happy. On very rare occasions, I get a whiff of Arpège, the perfume my mother wore, and it makes me both happy and sad.

God realizes that "the inclination of the human heart is evil from youth" (8:21), the same point that prompted the flood according to 6:5. We don't learn. Each generation says, "never again," and then the "again" happens. We speak of turning swords into plowshares, but we keep making bigger swords. We, as a collective—we, the human race—do not change; we let that evil inclination rule us. Yet God changes: God is the one who promises never again to blot out the world by flood. Isaiah 54:9-10 confirms this promise:

This is like the days of Noah to me:
Just as I swore that the waters of Noah
would never again go over the earth,
so I have sworn that I will not be angry with you
and will not rebuke you.
For the mountains may depart
and the hills be removed,
but my steadfast love shall not depart from you,
and my covenant of peace shall not be removed,
says the LORD, who has compassion on you.

Folks who like to talk about the Old Testament God of wrath have missed this and numerous other verses of divine compassion.

Given the human propensity for evil, we sometimes ask God to step in. However, we need to be careful in determining what we want. When God does step in, as the Book of Revelation describes, Noah's flood can look like a gentle drizzle. While in Genesis God promises not to destroy the world again by flood, later tradition creates a loophole. The spiritual "Oh Mary, Don't You Weep" contains the line, "God gave Noah the rainbow sign, no more water the fire next time." This verse is the origin of James Baldwin's 1963 classic, *The Fire Next Time*, a study of racism and religion. Sparking this imagery is 2 Peter 3:7, "But by the same word the present heavens and earth have been reserved for fire, being kept until the day of judgment and destruction of the godless." Whether that fire comes from God or from us (we might recall Hiroshima and Nagasaki) remains an open question.

The Covenant with Noah and His Sons

God repeats the message to "be fruitful and multiply and fill the earth" (1:28) to Noah and his sons (9:1, 7). It would have been nice for the text to mention Mrs. Noah and the wives of the sons (it's difficult to be fruitful and multiply on one's own). While the instructions to be good stewards of the earth remains, God now states, "Every moving thing that lives shall be food for you, and just as I gave you the green plants, I give you everything" (9:3). The earlier generations did not eat meat and therefore did not kill animals for food. Times have changed.

The only thing forbidden is consuming blood. In a convoluted sentence, God states, "For your own lifeblood I will surely require a reckoning: from every animal I will require it and from human beings, each one for the blood of another, I will require a reckoning for human life. Whoever sheds the blood of a human, / by a human shall that person's blood be shed, / for in his own image / God made humans" (9:5-6). Here's the first problem: a person who kills another is to be killed by a third party. But that third party is then guilty of shedding the blood of a human. By this chain of association, capital punishment cannot occur, for if it did, everyone would die.

The second problem concerns what we owe animals. While they are not in the divine image (see Genesis 1:26, a point reiterated here), their blood is also a source of life. Thus, a reckoning regarding the shedding of animal blood needs to be established. In Jewish tradition, any consumption of blood is forbidden: crack an egg and find a trace of blood, and the egg is not *kosher*, that is, fit for human consumption. The tradition of draining all blood from meat to make it kosher (the animal also has to be ritually slaughtered; the method is designed to alleviate as much pain as possible) is a reminder of the connection between life and blood. Deuteronomy 12:23 insists, "Only be sure that you do not eat the blood, for the blood is the life, and you shall not eat the life with the meat." Blood pudding is thus absolutely out of the question. (Not all Jews follow the dietary requirements, any more than all Christians follow the prohibition regarding consuming blood in Acts 15:29.)

While the New Testament document called the Epistle to the Hebrews concludes, "without the shedding of blood there is no forgiveness of sins" (Hebrews 9:22), this is not a Jewish view. Rather, God, who is the "Father of mercies," forgives freely, as Psalm 103:12-13 proclaims, "as far as the east is from the west, / so far he removes our transgressions from us. / As a father has compassion for his children, / so the LORD has compassion for those who fear him." The story of Jonah, another type of flood story, provides an excellent example of how repentance, rather than blood sacrifice, leads to divine mercy.

The covenant God establishes with all living creatures is that there will never again be a flood. Then the covenant is marked by a sign, just as circumcision will be the sign of the covenant made with Abraham: "I have set my bow in the clouds" (9:13). As we have noted, the bow is a weapon of war, as with "bow and arrow"; here, God turns the weapon of war into a sign of peace.

The covenant is universal, since Noah and his sons are, for the biblical narrative, the progenitors of all humans. The rainbow, whose ends cannot be found (leprechauns are still looking), encompasses all the earth.

Given that covenants typically have two parts, with each party contributing something, the rabbinic text *b. Sanhedrin* 56a records that God gave the descendants of Noah seven commandments. On the positive side, they are to establish courts of justice; for the negatives, no blaspheming Israel's God, no idolatry, no murder, no stealing, no sexual abuse, and no consumption of meat from a living animal. It is a fascinating exercise to determine, of all the laws we have, whether biblical or religious, state or national, what our top seven would be. In the aftermath of a disaster, when there is no system to enforce civility, what laws would we want to put into place?

The Vineyard

After naming the sons of Noah—Shem, Ham, and Japheth—and noting that Ham was the father of Canaan, the narrator observes, "Noah, a man of the soil, was the first to plant a vineyard" (9:20). The connection of Noah to the soil reminds us of Adam, charged to care for the garden but also one who had problems with forbidden fruit. It also reminds us of Cain, the agriculturalist, whose sacrifice was rejected and who was the first human to shed human blood. Yet concerning Noah, Genesis 5:29 announced that "out of the ground that the LORD has cursed this one shall bring us relief from work." Curses can be undone; curses can also become worse over the generations. Wine is good (1 Timothy 5:23 instructs, "No longer drink only water, but take a little wine for the sake of your stomach and your frequent ailments"); too much wine is not. Wine can be life-giving, but to an alcoholic, wine can be deadly.

Noah "drank some of the wine and became drunk, and he lay uncovered in his tent" (9:21). This story looks like a permutation of the garden of Eden: there, eating the fruit brought knowledge and so the need for clothing. Now, consumption of the fruit of the vine brings nudity and so the potential for shame. Wine can provide joy and relief; drunkenness can lead to humiliation; worse, it can lead to violence.

What happens next remains a matter of debate. Genesis 9:22 describes how "Ham, the father of Canaan," saw his father's nakedness and told his two brothers. The brothers drape a garment over their shoulders, walk backward into Noah's tent, and cover their father. Here's the problem: "When Noah awoke from his wine and knew what his youngest son had done to him" (Genesis 9:24), Noah curses not Ham but his son Canaan: "lowest of slaves shall he be to his brothers" (9:25).

What Ham did, other than looking, remains unclear. Cross-cultural mythology suggests that he "did" something other than just look, and what he did would have been castration. Zeus, for example, castrates his father, Saturn. Further, the Hebrew expression "to uncover the nakedness of one's father" means having sexual relations with one's mother. Leviticus 20:11 states, "The man who lies with his father's wife has uncovered his father's nakedness." The punishment for both parties is death. Or, perhaps Ham had sexual relations with his father. Leviticus 18 associates what it sees to be improper sexual behavior with the inhabitants of the land of Canaan ("You shall not do as they do in the land of Egypt, where you lived, and you shall not do as they do in the land of Canaan, to which I am bringing you.

You shall not follow their statutes" [Leviticus 18:3]), and Noah curses Canaan. There is no evidence from Canaanite texts that Canaanites were any more or less sexually immoral than ancient Israel. Rather, groups in the process of defining themselves typically cast aspersions, usually regarding diet and sexuality, on the behaviors of their opponents. *They* do what *we* would never do. This is how polemic works. Then, the polemic (this is what *they* do) can serve to justify attack.

The reception history of Genesis 9 is horrific. According to some early Jewish, Christian, and Muslim legends, on the ark, Ham, dogs, and ravens had sexual intercourse; this was forbidden, both morally (no celebration while people are dying) and practically (no room for more creatures). The punishment was to be blackened. The legend supported the Mid-Atlantic slave-trade; it continues to be promoted by white supremacists. One relatively recent example (out of many) of the effects of Genesis 9 comes from the lifetime of most of this book's readers, and it is something that most of the media ignored. In 1994, the Hutu population of Rwanda massacred approximately eight hundred thousand Tutsis, men, women, and children. Early tribal rivalry morphed into hatred when Europeans, mostly Dutch and German colonizers, taught that the Tutsis descended from Shem and the Hutu from Ham. The claim was based on the fake "racial science" of determining worth by measuring physical features such as nose and cranial size (the Nazis engaged in similar practices). This European racialized distinction, with its immoral social and economic implications, laid the groundwork first for the prioritizing of the Tutsi over the Hutu, and ultimately for the Hutu's uprising and revenge.

Myths can perdure. Our responsibility is to determine what lessons we learn from them. One approach is to remind ourselves of the horror of the flood rather than becoming desensitized by the nice children's stories. If our hearts can be open to empathy, we are in a better position to control our evil impulses. Another is to recognize that it was Noah, not God, who cursed Canaan, and Noah is not a great role model. What a man does after waking up from a bender should not be the determining factor in family, let alone national, relationships. Third, we can see in this story the impact the behavior of one generation has on another and then work to stop generational abuse. Fourth, we do well to remember that we are all related and thus the marginalization, enslavement, or genocide of one group by another should be seen as abhorrent.

Fifth, we recall that the text speaks with multiple voices. Noah curses Canaan, but God blesses everyone with the original covenant. God refuses to engage, ever again, in the violence of the flood. Ideally, people should do the same. In this story, God grieves and God regrets: if we are in the image of the divine, we should grieve when we see evil; we should regret actions that we have put in place that fail to do what is righteous, and then we should find better ways to correct the problems.

CHAPTER 4

The *Akedah* (The Near-Sacrifice of Isaac)

Genesis 22, God's testing of Abraham by commanding him to sacrifice his son, Isaac, is a major text in both Jewish and Christian thought. Jews read this passage, known as the *Akedah* (Hebrew for "binding," as Isaac was bound on the altar) in the synagogue on the second day of Rosh Hashanah, the Jewish new year. In some Christian tradition, Isaac's carrying the wood for his own sacrifice foreshadows the death of Jesus. Many Christians read Genesis 22 on Good Friday or for the Easter vigil. The passage raises questions about theodicy (why would God command such a horrific thing?), fidelity (did Abraham pass the test?), responsibility (what did Isaac know, and when did he know it?), secrecy (what does Sarah know?), and more.

The *Akedah* is one of my favorite passages, and after well over half a century of thinking about it, I am still puzzled by, amazed by, and even inspired by its words.

After These Things

Genesis 22:1 begins "After these things." Translations that offer "Some time later" (NIV) or "Sometime afterward" (NABRE) do not get at the pathos of the opening. These "things" are not simply a temporal transition. The specific "things" are the expulsions of Hagar and her son Ishmael in the previous chapter. Jews read Genesis 21:1-34 on the first day of Rosh Hashanah and Genesis 22:1-24 on the second day. The two stories form a diptych of parents and children, sacrifice and salvation.

According to Genesis 21:9, Sarah "saw the son of Hagar the Egyptian, whom she had borne to Abraham, playing with her son Isaac." Sarah never addresses Hagar directly, and the identification "the Egyptian" distinguishes Hagar from Abraham and Sarah, who are from Mesopotamia. More problematic is how to translate the Hebrew *mitzachek*, which the NRSVue renders as "playing." The word is a play on the name "Isaac" (Hebrew: *yitzchok*), which means "laughter," so "playing" is not a bad translation.

Exacerbating the translation problem is that the phrase "with her son Isaac" does not appear in the Hebrew. It appears in the Septuagint and other early translations. Thus, we can speculate as to why Sarah found Ishmael's "playing" a problem. Since the term *mtizachek* appears elsewhere with a connotation of sexual enjoyment, perhaps of an inappropriate kind, she might have seen Ishmael as a sexual predator. Genesis 26:8 notes that Abimelech, the king of the Philistines, "looked out of a window and saw [Isaac] *mitzachek*ing [NRSVue "fondling"] his wife Rebekah." Isaac had told Abimelech that Rebekah was his sister, so Abimelech is, appropriately, shocked. Similarly, in Genesis 39:14, Potiphar's wife, whose sexual advances Joseph rebuffed, "called out to the members of her household and said to them, 'See, he [NRSVue "my husband"] has brought among us a Hebrew *l'tzachek* [NRSVue "to insult"] us!" (We'll circle back to Mrs. Potiphar and Joseph in chapter 6 of this study.)

I do not bring up these subjects to be titillating. I bring them up because the Bible is honest in telling us that sexual abuse occurs, even in the best of families. Moreover, the Bible shows us that charges of sexual abuse are a potent means of castigating people who are "not us." It is this type of ethnic prejudice that the Egyptian Mrs. Potiphar uses against the Hebrew Joseph. And even more, what is innocent play (e.g., friendly banter, a pat on the shoulder, a light flirtation) for one person may be to another a form of harassment or sexual aggression.

Or, for one more possibility, perhaps Sarah saw Ishmael "playing with" Isaac, not in any prurient way but in the roughhouse ways that boys sometimes play. Her little son Isaac is growing up; he is developing the knowledge of good and evil that comes with leaving infancy behind, and he is making his own choices. Perhaps he wants to spend more time with big brother Ishmael, and Sarah can't let go. Perhaps the big brother, who is good at sports, is more interesting to him than his mother, who is always concerned to protect him.

Sarah tells Abraham, "Cast out this slave woman with her son, for the son of this slave woman shall not inherit along with my son Isaac" (21:10). She does not use the name "Hagar"; she sees her only as the "slave woman." We'll encounter this same sort of labeling when we meet Mrs. Potiphar, the Egyptian who seeks to remove from her house the "Hebrew slave" Joseph. Ignored by her words is the fact that this unnamed son, Ishmael, is also Abraham's firstborn. Ignored as well is 16:3, which recounts, "Sarai, Abram's wife, took Hagar the Egyptian, her slave, and gave her to her husband Abram as a wife." *As a wife!*

While "the matter [NRSVue; Hebrew *davar*, the same term that appears in Genesis 22:1, a "thing"] was very distressing to Abraham on account of his son" (21:10), he says nothing in response—no mention that it was Sarah who arranged Ishmael's conception in the first place. Nor does Abraham show any concern for Hagar. At this point, I'm happy with neither Abraham nor Sarah.

God tells Abraham, "Do not be distressed because of the boy [Hebrew *na'ar*; we'll come back to this term] and because of your slave woman; whatever Sarah says to you, do as she tells you, for it is through Isaac that offspring shall be named for you. As for the son of the slave woman, I will make a nation of him also, because he is your offspring" (21:12-13). I would have preferred that God name Hagar, as Hagar had named God as the "God who sees" in 16:13. I would have preferred that Abraham, who in Genesis 19 argued for the sparing of Sodom and Gomorrah should ten righteous people be found, argue that Hagar and Ishmael be spared. On the other hand, we cannot know what Hagar or Ishmael was thinking. Did they rejoice that they would finally be free, or did they wish to remain in the camp where they had food and shelter? Were they leaving Eden, or were they leaving hell?

"Abraham rose early in the morning and took bread and a skin of water and gave it to Hagar, putting it on her shoulder, along with the child, and sent her away" (21:14). He will in the next chapter again rise early in the morning and prepare for the trip; this time he will put wood on Isaac's shoulder. Hagar will face the prospect of her son dying in the wilderness, and she cries out on his behalf. Abraham, ready to sacrifice his son, does not cry out. While "God heard the voice" of Ishmael (21:17, a play on the name Ishmael, which means "God hears") and comes to his rescue by revealing a well to Hagar, Isaac does not cry out from the altar to which his father bound him. God will rescue both sons, but at what cost to them and to their parents?

Genesis 22 begins "After these things. . . ." We do not know how many days or years passed after Abraham expelled Ishmael and Hagar. Genesis 21:8 notes that Isaac had just been weaned, so we can imagine he was about three years old. Immediately following this verse is the comment about Ishmael's "playing." We now have the question: How old is Isaac at the *Akedah*? Isaac could be a child, as Christian tradition typically portrays him. He could also be thirty-seven, which is the rabbinic reading (*Genesis Rabbah* 56). The rabbis arrive at this age by mathematics. When she was ninety, Sarah gave birth to Isaac (17:17). She died at age 127 (23:1), and her death notice comes immediately after the *Akedah*. If she died because of the *Akedah* (see the following discussion), then Isaac must be 127 minus 90, or 37 years old. How we interpret Genesis 22 will depend in part on the level of maturity we grant Isaac.

"After these things" also means *everything that came before*: creation, the events in the garden of Eden, Cain and Abel, the flood, the Tower of Babel, and Abraham's call. Each time we frame the story differently, we may arrive at a different reading. We can look to our past to see how we came to where we are. If we can name those times when we prevailed, when we succeeded or stayed the course, we are likely to be stronger the next time difficulties occur.

God Tested Abraham

The testing motif can be found implicitly in Genesis 3, the story of Eden's forbidden tree. We can sense it in God's comment to Cain about the need to master sin. It is explicit at Sinai when Moses instructs the people, "Do not be afraid, for God has come only to test you and to put the fear of him upon you so that you do not sin" (Exodus 20:20). Psalm 11:5 states that "the LORD tests the righteous and the wicked." Paul writes, "No testing has overtaken you that is not common to everyone. God is faithful, and he will not let you be tested beyond your strength, but with the testing he will also provide the way out so that you may be able to endure it" (1 Corinthians 10:13). Since God knows what is in our hearts, the tests are not proof *to God* of anything. Such tests tell us something about ourselves. Do we face difficulty, or do we flee? Do we act on behalf of someone else or on our own behalf? Do we take the wide path, the easy way one, when the narrow path leads to righteousness? Tests can also reveal to us our own abilities and our own knowledge, and passing a test can lead to a sense of inner peace or internal strength. Tests can also reveal weaknesses that require attention, leading to self-improvement. Not all tests are bad.

Regarding Abraham, it is not clear to me why this test was needed since he seems to have a pretty good sense of his fidelity. When God asks him, "Go from your country and your kindred and your father's house to the land that I will show you" (12:1), Abraham goes. When God sets circumcision as the sign of the covenant, Abraham complies. When God tells him to comply with Sarah's demand and expel his wife Hagar and son Ishmael, Abraham gets up early to follow through. Rabbinic midrash suggests that Abraham passed ten tests.

Perhaps then his tests are for us. Would we obey? Would we question? Do we only follow orders? Could we, would we, do what Abraham did?

The notion of the divine test appears again in Job 1–2. Job, who is blameless, faces property loss, then the deaths of his children and then physical pain, all as a test from "the satan" (Hebrew, "the accuser," a member of the heavenly court, one of the "sons of God") to see whether he will deny God. Job rails—his famous silence lasts only for the first two chapters—and calls for justice.

In the New Testament, Satan (here a proper name) "tests" or "tempts" (the terms are the same in Greek) Jesus in the wilderness (Matthew 4:1-11; Luke 4:1-13). The famous "Lead us not into temptation" (KJV) can also be translated "Do not bring us to the test" or "Do not bring us to the time of trial" (Matthew 6:13; Luke 11:4). James 1:3 states that "the testing of your faith produces endurance" (personally, I could do without such tests). James 1:13 also states, "No one, when tempted, should say, 'I am being tempted by God,' for God cannot be tempted by evil and he himself tempts no one." Comments such as "God brings you no burden you cannot bear" or Nietzche's *Was mich nicht umbringt, macht mich starker* ("What doesn't kill me makes me stronger") I find of little comfort. Testing in the classroom determines whether we know the material; testing in the medical lab can show whether we need new pills or infusions. These situations are not comparable to being asked to sacrifice one's child or to determining whether one's theology is unwavering. To blame misfortune on God may seek to find meaning and thus justification in something that is meaningless. As with the flood, we may be better shifting our questions from "Why did *God* do this?" to "What do *I* do now?"

We read that "God tested Abraham." The test is also for anyone who would read Genesis 22. What would we do if we were in Abraham's sandals? Were God to ask me to kill my child, any child, I would hope my response would be something along the lines of "Why have you forsaken me?" (Psalm 22:1) or "Hear my voice, O God, in my complaint" (Psalm 64:1) or "Shall not the Judge of all the earth do what is just?" (Genesis 18:25) rather than "Sir, yes, sir."

He Said to Him, "Abraham!" And He Said, "Here I Am."

The first verse of the *Akedah* (22:1) concludes with first a summons and then a response. God (Hebrew *Elohim*) calls, "Abraham!" This is the new name God gave him: "No longer shall your name be Abram ["exalted father" or "exalted ancestor"], but your name shall be Abraham ["father of many" or "father of a multitude"] for I have made you the ancestor of a multitude of nations" (17:5). The name suggests progeny. Abraham knows that concerning his firstborn son, Ishmael, God "will make a nation of him also, because he is your offspring" (21:13). Yet Abraham does not know whether he will ever see Ishmael again. Rabbinic sources, seeking to wrap up the story of Hagar, propose that after Sarah dies, Abraham remarries Hagar, who also goes by the name Keturah (see Genesis 25:1-2, 4; 1 Chronicles 1:32-33). The next time we see Ishmael, whose mother Hagar had taken him to Egypt to find him a wife among her own people, is when he returns to Canaan to reunite with Isaac and bury their father's body. By calling upon Abraham by name, God is reminding him that his lineage will continue.

Abraham's response, "Here I am" (Hebrew: *hineni*), is more than a "here" or "present" in the sense of responding to a roll call. A few translations offer "Ready" or "Yes," which makes a significant term banal. "At your service" and "Happy to help" don't work either. The Hebrew is "Here" (for KJV aficionados, "Behold") plus the first-person suffix: "Behold, me." "See me" or "Here I am." *Hineni* connotes being present in the fullest sense. It also serves as a theme throughout the chapter. When Isaac calls his father, Abraham responds *hineni* (22:7). When the angel calls to Abraham, Abraham responds *hineni* (22:11). We hear the refrain again multiple times in the Bible. When Isaac calls to Esau, "My son," Esau responds, *hineni* (27:1). When Jacob, pretending to be his brother Esau, calls to his father, Isaac responds, *hineni* (27:18). An angel calls to Jacob in a dream, and he responds, *hineni* (31:11). Jacob commissions Joseph to find his brothers, and Joseph responds, *hineni* (37:13). So Jacob responds to God in 46:2; so Moses responds to God at the burning bush in Exodus 3:4. The refrain marks 1 Samuel 3, the call of Samuel.

Hineni reminds us of what it means to be focused: Here I am, without any of the clutter or distraction, as we should be fully present to our children, our partners, people who demand or need our attention. When God calls, we stop, and we listen. It should be the same when our children call. No "Let me finish this email" or "As soon as the song is over" or "After the third strike." Instead, we are to respond, "Here I am. I am not distracted; I am fully attentive to you. What do you need?"

"Take Your Son"

"He said, 'Take your son, your only son Isaac, whom you love, and go to the land of Moriah and offer him there as a burnt offering on one of the mountains that I shall show you.'" Genesis 22:2 is one of the Bible's most terrifying verses. Hebrew prose is relatively condensed, especially compared to Greek texts such as Homer's *Iliad* and *Odyssey*. But this verse appears, on first read, redundant. God simply could have said, "Take Isaac." As it moves toward greater specificity—son, only son, beloved son, Isaac—it shows an increasing focus on this one special child.

In Hebrew, following the verb for "take" is the particle *na*, which means something like "please" but also connotes urgency. It appears first in Genesis 12:11, where Abraham, relocating to Egypt because of food insecurity in Canaan, says to Sarah, "I know well that you are a woman beautiful in appearance." Missing from this NRSVue translation is Abraham's opening comment in Hebrew, *Hine-nah,* "Look, please" or "Behold, please." The text continues, "Say you are my sister, so that it may go well with me because of you and that my life may be spared on your account" (12:13). The "say" is *imri-nah*, "say please." These are not simply requests; they are matters of life and death. Behold! Look! Pay attention! Please! Most readers will know the particle from the invocation, Hosanna (Hebrew *hoshia-nah*), meaning "Save please" or "Save now."

Next, the term in 22:2 translated "only" as in "your only son" also has the sense of "precious" or "dear." The New Jewish Publication Society translates it as "favored one." We see this connotation in Proverbs 4:3, which reads, "When I was a son with my father, / tender and my mother's *favorite*": beneath the NRSVue's "favorite" is the term translated "only" for Genesis 22:2. The Septuagint translates the Hebrew term in question as *agapetos*, "beloved." Here is one of the multiple reasons why many Christians came to see the *Akedah* as prefiguring the story of Jesus, proclaimed in the New Testament as the only son, the beloved son, of God the Father.

The same Hebrew term for "only" with a sense of "beloved" appears in Judges 11, another story about a child sacrifice. However, in Judges 11, God gives no command to offer the child, and no angel comes to the rescue. Jephthah, the son of a concubine, cast out of his house by his half-brothers, seeks a sense of personal worth while consistently sabotaging himself. On the eve of a battle, he vows to sacrifice "whatever" or "whoever" (the Hebrew could go either way) first comes out of his house to celebrate his victory. Suggestions that he was thinking of the family dog are not of much help. Judges 11:34 reports, "Then Jephthah came to his home at Mizpah, and there was his daughter coming out to meet him with timbrels and with dancing. She was his *only* child; he had no son or daughter except her" (emphasis added). The story of Jepthah and his daughter increases the pathos of the *Akedah*. The connections also raise other questions, not only about rash vows but also about how our actions impact our children and how children respond to a parent's problematic actions. Jephthah is a tragic figure, as is his daughter; Abraham and Isaac may be as well.

The NRSVue translates Genesis 22:2 as "your son, your only son Isaac, whom you love," which is not the Hebrew word order. The Hebrew offers, "your son, your only [son], whom you love, Isaac," so that the naming is the climax. In contrast, Jephthah's daughter receives no name. From this protracted introduction, the rabbis imagine a conversation between God and Abraham in which Abraham, aware of what is coming (no one wants to be tested), attempts to escape. "Take your son," says God. "I have two sons: Ishmael and Isaac," responds Abraham. "Therefore, I cannot follow your instructions." God specifies, "Your only son." Abraham counters, "I have only one with Hagar and only one with Sarah." "The one you love," adds God. At this point, Abraham admits that he loves Ishmael, the son whom he expelled. He also admits that he loves Isaac, who to this point has been the focus of

Sarah's attention. Only upon affirming that he loves them both does God specify, "Isaac."

God does not simply say, "Go"; he tells Abraham, "Go you" or, in better English, "You go." The Hebrew *lech lecha* appears one other time in the Bible. According to Genesis 12:1, "The Lord said to Abram, '*lech lecha* from your country. . . .'" First, Abraham must uproot from his home and so from his past; now he must uproot his family by killing his son and so being cut off from the future. In the first, he goes from; in the second, he goes *to*. Both times, Abraham trusts in divine providence.

Genesis 12:1 is God's first address to Abraham; Genesis 22:16 is his last (an angel, not God, stops the sacrifice). In both settings, Abraham builds an altar. When we look at the two verses together, we may be prompted to ask, "From where have I come?" and "To where am I going?" In Genesis 16:8, an angel asks Hagar, fleeing from Sarah's abuse, "Where have you come from and where are you going?" We are stronger when we can answer both questions. The past has shaped us, but we are not restricted to it. The future is open, but it will also always somehow be tied to the past. The present is what we make it.

God tells Abraham to offer Isaac as a "whole burnt offering," consumed completely by the fire. In animal sacrifices, parts of the animal are consumed by fire, and other parts are eaten by the one offering the sacrifice, usually together with the family. The text evokes Abel, the first person to offer a blood sacrifice, and Noah, who made this type of offering upon exiting the ark. Echoes continue: Will Isaac die as Abel died? Is Abraham in the role of Cain? We realize that the *Akedah* is connected to the flood with such concerns as the family line in danger; the vague "mountains that I shall show you" here in Genesis 22:2 and the vague "mountains of Ararat" in 8:4; Noah cursing his grandson and that child's posterity and a father willing to endanger a child.

The *Akedah* is popularly read as the rejection of child sacrifice. It's a good and ancient reading, but I'm not sure this is why the story was initially told. If it were, Jephthah didn't get the notice (Judges 11). Following the conquest of Jericho, Joshua states, "Cursed before the Lord be anyone who tries / to rebuild this city. . . . / At the cost of his firstborn he shall lay its foundation, / and at the cost of his youngest he shall set up its gates!" (Joshua 6:26). The curse is fulfilled according to 1 Kings 16:34.

Other biblical passages explicitly reject child sacrifice. Leviticus 18:21 is adamant, "You shall not give any of your offspring to sacrifice them to Molech and so profane the name of your God." Deuteronomy 18:10 reiterates, "No one shall be found among you who makes a son or daughter pass through fire." Micah 6:7 asks, "Shall I give my firstborn for my transgression, / the fruit of my body for the sin of my soul?" The next verse is the famous line, "He has told you, O mortal, what is good, / and what does the Lord require of you / but to do justice and to love kindness / and to walk humbly with your God?" (Micah 6:8). For the Bible, child sacrifice is generally indicative of worshipping gods other than the God of Israel. King Ahaz of Judah, one of the "bad" kings, "even made his son pass through fire, according to the abominable practices of the nations whom the Lord had driven out before the people of Israel" (2 Kings 16:3).

In one of the Bible's weirder passages (which is saying something), the prophet Ezekiel (20:26) speaks of God giving the people impossible laws: "I defiled them through their very gifts, in their offering up all their firstborn, in order that I might horrify them, so that they might know that I am the Lord." For Ezekiel, child sacrifice is appalling. It should be hard to imagine anything more horrific than killing one's child.

Jeremiah 19:5 condemns the people of Judah who built "the high places of Baal [a Canaanite god] to burn their children in the fire as burnt offerings to Baal, which I [i.e., God] did not command or decree, nor did it enter my mind." Glossing this verse, with its triple denial—command, decree, did not enter my mind—the Babylonian Talmud (*Ta'anit* 4a) fills in the details: "did not command" is the rejection of the sacrifice by Mesha the king of Moab of his firstborn during a battle (2 Kings 3:27); "decree" concerns Jephthah's sacrifice of his daughter (Judges 11), and "did not enter my mind" is the *Akedah*. Thus, for the rabbis, by no means did God intend that Abraham sacrifice his son.

These numerous references can help us to think not only about the purpose of "sacrifice" but also about our children. For example, do we sacrifice our children by enjoining them to pursue military service? Do we think of the jobs that put people in danger—police, firefighters, or special forces—as possibly leading to self-sacrifice? Do we promote martyrs or martyrdom, and if so, what do we see as worth our lives or the lives of our children? Do we teach our children to speak out for what they believe, even if such public statements can lead to imprisonment or martyrdom? Do we model such behavior ourselves? Should we?

Finally, still on the second verse of Genesis 22, we hear of the "land of Moriah." It has not been mentioned previously. Only in 2 Chronicles 3:1, one of the latest Hebrew biblical books, do we learn, "Solomon began to build the house of the Lord in Jerusalem on Mount Moriah." These two verses are the only biblical references to Moriah. Thus, the site of the *Akedah* is Mount Zion, the site of the Jerusalem Temple. In Jewish tradition (*Targum Pseudo-Jonathan*), the location is also the site of Noah's altar. According to the Church Father Eusebius, the site of Isaac's binding is the site of Jesus's crucifixion.

The Septuagint translates the Hebrew *moriah* as "high" or, for a more biblical-sounding term, "lofty." The name could also mean "of the Amorites," a group that appears about eighty times in the Bible, often alongside "Canaanites." Or, the name means something like "my teacher (Hebrew *moreh*) is Yah" (as in *YHWH*). "Moriah" also sounds like "Moreh". There God told Abraham, "To your offspring I will give this land," and Abraham "built there an altar to the LORD, who had appeared to him" (12:6-7). Abraham's first sacrifice is thanksgiving for progeny and land; the *Akedah* threatens both.

Abraham could have sacrificed Isaac anywhere. Genesis has no restriction on where an altar can be built. Only with the reign of King Josiah, about a thousand years later, was sacrifice limited to Jerusalem. Why then the three-day journey to Moriah? I like to think that the distant location was first designed to spare Sarah. I suspect that Sarah, who yearned for this child, nursed this child, loved this child, would have protested, "God forbid it! This must never happen!" (see Matthew 16:22). More, the journey gives everyone involved time to reflect: to turn back, to flee, to question, to dissuade, to hope for another message from heaven.

The Journey

God commands Abraham to sacrifice his beloved son, and according to Genesis 22:3, he rises early to fulfill the task! Traditionally, the notice indicates his fidelity: he sets aside his own sense of morality to fulfill God's commandment. But this temporal notice is also an echo of Genesis 21:14, "Abraham rose early in the morning and took bread and a skin of water and gave it to Hagar, putting it on her shoulder, along with the child, and sent her away." Hagar and Ishmael also rose early that morning. Hagar, too, must risk the life of her son, and she, too, like Abraham, does not protest. Claims that she could say nothing because she was enslaved do not hold: enslaved people speak. In trying to imagine Hagar's perspective, we may get better purchase on Abraham: Has she hope? Hope against hope? Can she trust in God's mercy? Can she trust in her own resilience? What can she do to protect her son? What will happen to her and to her son because of these events? How will they each remember what happened? How will they live into their freedom in their own homeland?

Genesis 22:3 continues: Abraham "saddled his donkey, and took two of his young men with him and his son Isaac; he cut the wood for the burnt offering." Why the two young men? Abraham cut the wood himself (good for someone over one hundred years old); Isaac could have helped with the donkey and the provisions. Perhaps Abraham needs someone to corroborate his account of what happened to Isaac. Or perhaps he wants company on the long journey home.

The young men are not needed for the plot; like Rosencrantz and Guildenstern or Tweedledum and Tweedledee, they are interchangeable. They do not speak; the narrator records no reaction from them. But for the story itself, they present a fascinating contrast with Isaac. The Hebrew term translated "young man" is *na'ar*; it connotes a male who is not a child but who is still under someone else's authority, whether son or servant or enslaved. Abraham uses the same term for Isaac, although the NRSVue hides the connection by translating 22:5 as "Abraham said to his young men (*na'arav*), 'Stay here with the donkey; the boy (*na'ar*) and I will go over there.'" There is no necessary reason to translate the first use as "young men" and the second, in the same verse, as "boy." The NRSVue winds up infantilizing Isaac as a "boy" rather than describing him as a "young man," and thus, by implication, it makes him more a victim and less an active participant. Next, by using the same term for the two young men as for Isaac, Abraham suggests a solidarity among the three. On the one hand, they are about the same age, and they were raised in the same household; on the other, two are servants, and one is the heir. What sort of relationship do they have? Third, from a distance, all three are, more or less, the same: Do we judge people differently because of their parentage or their status? As for the two young men, did *they* wonder about the lack of the sacrificial animal? Should they have followed Abraham and, given what they see, attempted to stop him? Do they think that if perhaps the heir dies, they might inherit Abraham's estate? Finally, do *we* act if we suspect something is awry, or do we think, "That's none of my business"?

When I was an undergraduate (Noah was still on the ark), I read Christian philosopher Søren Kierkegaard's 1843 work, *Fear and Trembling.* Kierkegaard casts Abraham as the "knight of faith" who took "a leap of faith" by engaging in the "teleological suspension of the ethical." Otherwise put, the end (Greek: *telos*) justifies the means, even if the means run counter to our sense of morality. This argument made no sense to me. My first thought was that people who believe they are called by God to kill their children are not knights of faith; they are in need of psychiatric intervention.

Yet there may be occasions when confession trumps ethics. Here are two examples from the past, with tragic contemporary echoes. First, from late antiquity, the Babylonian Talmud (*b. Gittin* 57b) glosses a story recorded in the Jewish-Hellenistic texts 2 and 4 Maccabees (canonical for Catholic and Orthodox Christians but not for Jews or Protestants). In this account, a widowed mother watched her seven sons be tortured to death by the Syrian-Greek king Antiochus IV Epiphanes for refusing to violate the Torah's commands against idol worship. The mother tells her last child, as he is being led to his death, "My son, go and say to your father Abraham, 'You bound one son to the altar, but I bound seven altars.'" In effect, she sacrifices her children by encouraging them to persevere through the pain instead of going through the motions of committing idolatry and so saving their lives. They, and finally she, all die rather than violate divine commands.

Second, in the year 1190, twenty-four years after the Norman Conquest of Britain, a Christian mob in York, England, attacked the local Jewish community. The Jewish families sought protection in the

"King's Tower" (today, Clifford's Tower), and when they realized they could not hold out, on March 16, the Sabbath before Passover, the father of each family killed his wife and his children, and then the men committed suicide rather than have the Christian mob kill them or perhaps, kill the parents, baptize the children, and raise them as Christians.

The *Akedah* poses difficult questions: For what cause would I give my life? For what cause would I sacrifice my children? Given the option of "sin or die" or "convert or die," which do we choose?

According to Genesis 22:4, "on the third day Abraham looked up and saw the place far away." Two verses ago, God spoke of the place that "I shall show you." Now Abraham finds the place on his own. Where does God's command stop and Abraham's interpretation begin?

The third day is also a biblical trope, appearing in both Testaments forty times, that begins here. Among other references are the appearance of God on Mount Sinai (Exodus 19:11), the day Esther petitions King Ahasuerus to spare her people (Esther 5:1), a day of being raised up (Hosea 6:2), and the day of Jesus's resurrection (1 Corinthians 15:4). It is time to think about what we are about to do and time to think of what we have done. We might stop to think, "What was I doing three days ago?" or "What am I doing three days hence?"

Abraham orders the young men to remain with the donkey while he and Issac—the *na'ar*, the young man—"will go over there; we will worship [literally "prostrate ourselves"], and then we will come back to you" (22:5). Might the two young men be thinking: "Wish I were Isaac, the heir," so that we, too, could worship with Abraham? Or were they wondering about Ishmael, also a *na'ar* and perhaps their friend? Or were they wondering *what* would be sacrificed, since Abraham did not bring along an animal for the offering?

Father and Son

Abraham takes the wood and places it on "his son Isaac" while he carries "the fire" (likely a flint) and the knife. Again, the drumbeat of "his son." The verse adds, "the two of them walked on together" (22:6). There is unity of purpose: two, going in the same direction, sharing the material needed for the sacrifice. Terms like "his son" and "together" reinforce the closeness. We know that Abraham grieved over the loss of Ishmael; here we get a sense that he is also close to this other "son whom [he] loves."

Isaac's carrying the wood comes to be understood by Christians as a prefiguration of Jesus—another beloved son handed over by his father to death—carrying his cross. The analogy is not strained. *Genesis Rabbah*, a midrashic collection dating to the fourth and fifth centuries CE, compares Isaac bearing the wood to be used for his death to a condemned person who is forced to carry the gibbet on which he is to be hanged. The scene also recalls Ishmael, placed by Abraham on Hagar's shoulders (21:14).

Finally, Isaac speaks. How we picture him—as a child (one common Christian view; see Caravaggio's painting) or an adult of thirty-seven (a rabbinic take; see Rembrandt's painting)—impacts how we, with Isaac, take the next steps. He calls "to his father Abraham" (22:7). No need to repeat "father." Repetition continues as Isaac addresses Abraham, "Father!" Abraham responds to Isaac as he did to God, *hineni*, "Here I am," and he adds, "my son." Now the question. Isaac asks, "The fire and the wood are here, but where is the lamb for a burnt offering?"

The term translated "lamb" is the generic term for "sheep," so lamb is the translator's choice. Isaac could be a child who asks out of innocence. He could be an adult who knows what his father intends and is seeking an honest answer. He may be a victim, an enabler, or responsible for his own fate. I am intrigued by the idea that Isaac, the child of an elderly mother, may have developmental disabilities but is dearly loved by his parents, by Rebekah, the wife Abraham's servant (and God, as behind-the-scenes matchmaker) chose for him, and by his twins Esau and Jacob. There is no wrong answer here: as with Abraham, there are choices.

Abraham's response can be interpreted in several ways depending on how we punctuate it. Ancient Hebrew manuscripts lack punctuation (it had not yet been invented). My friend Marc Brettler likes to demonstrate the importance of punctuation with the distinction between "Let's eat, grandma" and "Let's eat grandma." In the NRSVue, Genesis 22:8a reads, "Abraham said, 'God himself will provide the lamb for a burnt offering, [*comma*] my son.'" In this reading, Abraham assures Isaac that God will provide the lamb. The text could also be punctuated, "God himself will provide the lamb for a burnt offering: [*colon*] my son." In this reading, Abraham specifies that Isaac *is* the burnt offering whom God provides. Or, perhaps Abraham hopes that God will provide an alternative to the test.

The Hebrew behind "will provide" is, literally, "will see for himself." A moment of etymological nerdiness (I love this stuff!): "provide" comes from the Latin *pro* (forward, in front, before) and *videre* (to see, as in "video"). The word "provision" makes the connection clearer. The Hebrew expression anticipates Genesis 22:14, where Abraham names the place of the offering *YHWH-yireh,* or "The Lord Will Provide." We're happy with the God who provides, but what are we to make of a God who tests? Genesis 22 gives both depictions.

Isaac does not respond. Rather, in silence (we readers can fill in a conversation), "the two of them walked on together" (22:8b). The word for "together" is the same as "as one." They are united in motion;

whether they are united in purpose depends upon how we understand both father and son.

The Sacrifice

"When they came to the place that God had shown him" (22:9a), the time for the trial is upon them. Abraham acts: he builds an altar, stacks wood carefully for burning the offering, and then he "bound his son Isaac and laid him on the altar on top of the wood" (22:9b). *His son Isaac*—the repetition enhances the pathos. Isaac says nothing. He may be shocked, confused, or resigned. He may have faith to match, even outdo, what his father displays. He may trust that help will come at the last minute, whether his father will relent or a voice from heaven will stop his father's hand. *Genesis Rabbah* 56.8 depicts Isaac, fully aware and fully on board, telling his father to bind him tightly lest he flinch and so invalidate the sacrifice.

The Hebrew for "bound," *akad* (whence *Akedah*), appears only here in the Tanakh with the meaning "bind." There are several explanations for why the author uses this term rather than more common words for making an offering or tying up an animal, but my preference is to take an allegorical meaning here: only this one time, and never again, will God issue such a command.

"Abraham reached out his hand and took the knife to kill [better: "to slaughter," as with a kosher animal] his son" (22:10). He would have done it. God commanded, and he obeyed. He could be Kierkegaard's knight of faith. He could be deranged. He may even be testing God.

The Rescue

At the last minute, an "angel of the Lord" calls from heaven (22:11). Not God, but an angel. Source critics explain that the first part of the story, which uses the Hebrew *Elohim* for God, comes from the E source, a product of the Northern Kingdom of Israel that was destroyed by the Assyrians in 722 BCE. It was then edited by people in Judah, the Southern Kingdom, who used the term *YHWH* (translated as "the LORD"). Could be. But ancient readers were not source critics. They found other explanations for the shift in the designation. My literary takeaway is that God did not want to respond directly because Abraham failed the test. In my reading, Abraham should have pleaded for the life of his son. Feel free to disagree.

I am intrigued by the idea that Abraham is also testing God. Biblical texts frequently insist that God not be "put to the test" (e.g., Deuteronomy 6:16; Psalm 78; Judith 8:12-13; Wisdom 1:3; Matthew 4:7). God wants to know about Abraham's fidelity; Abraham may be wondering the same about God. Even today, we "test" God: we engage in actions that we know God would find less than ideal; we sin by omission as well as commission; we say "not my problem" rather than "what can I do to help?" Sometimes we make rash vows, as did Jephthah: "If you help me with this, then I will give to charity, stop smoking, lower my cholesterol, rein in my temper. . . ."

The angel calls, "Abraham, Abraham!"; the repetition indicates urgency. In Exodus 3:4, the angel from the burning bush calls, "Moses, Moses!" The address "Samuel! Samuel!" marks the prophet's commission in 1 Samuel 3:4. Jesus says, "Martha, Martha," before telling her that her sister Mary has chosen the better portion (Luke 10:41). In Acts 9:4, Jesus calls, "Saul, Saul, why do you persecute me?" People of a certain age will also remember *The Brady Bunch*'s "Marcia, Marcia, Marcia!" Since "Abraham" means "father of many," the repetition is ironic: kill your son and your posterity through Isaac is lost.

Abraham responds, "*Hineni*, here I am" (22:11b). First to God, then to his son Isaac, and now to the angel: he is ever-present. It was not that long ago when Abraham responded, "*Hineni*, here I am" to Isaac, right before (not) answering the question about the lamb. Isaac is still bound on the altar. If he had called out from there, would his father have answered?

The angel commands, "Do not lay your hand on the boy" and adds "or do anything to him" (22:12a). The midrash wonders about the addition. One interpretation suggests that Abraham was so committed to what God demanded of him that he needed to be told twice to stop.

Then the angel explains that Abraham passed the test, "for now I know that you fear God, since you have not withheld your son, your only son, from me" (22:12b). "Fear" in the biblical sense does not mean "scared"; it means struck with awe. God is not supposed to be "scary" any more than parents should be "scary." One midrash, likely wondering why this angel is suddenly speaking for God, suggests that the test was for the angels, who doubted Abraham's fidelity. This is the same plot that begins the Book of Job, where Job's testing is to prove to the satan that Job's faith is not dependent on his good fortune. Rather than see Job and Abraham as victims of a test designed to make a point to doubting angels in the heavenly court, I'd prefer to see them as offering possible responses to impossible situations.

That the angel, speaking for God, states, "Now I know that you fear God" can indicate that God really did not know what was in Abraham's heart. Biblical stories vary on the extent of divine omniscience. If God knows everything, then God cannot be surprised. I'd prefer to think that God leaves the future open and so can both delight in our good deeds and mourn our failures.

Still others suggest that the test was for Abraham's benefit: Could he continue to follow a God who not only blesses but also tests, who not only rewards but also demands? Could Abraham acknowledge the divine freedom manifest both in choosing him and granting him a son and a covenant and in testing him by first telling him to expel his first-born, Ishmael, and then commanding him to sacrifice Isaac?

The *Akedah*, and indeed most of Genesis, asks, over and over, what kind of God do we want? One who keeps us as innocents and infants or one who gives us free will? One who punishes or rewards, or both? One who watches over us or one who keeps a naughty-and-nice tally? One who knows all or one who can be surprised?

Serendipitously, Abraham looks up and sees "a ram, caught in a thicket by its horns" (22:13). He sacrifices the ram instead of his son. Most people I know do not use "thicket" in regular conversation: it means a dense growth of trees, bushes, or thorns. For fans of archaeology, "ram in a thicket" is the technical term for matching figurines, dating from ca. 2600–2400 BCE, found by archaeologists at Ur (yes, that Ur, Abraham's home; today, southern Iraq). One is in the British Museum, and the other is owned by the University of Pennsylvania. We do not know whether the artifacts are products of a story; perhaps the *Akedah*, like the flood, had other ancient versions.

As for the ram, whether it was God's plan to have Abraham offer the ram instead of Isaac or whether Abraham came up with the idea on his own remains unstated. On the practical level, Abraham has already constructed an altar, and offering the ram will ensure Isaac's safety. One midrash proposes that on the sixth day, right before the Sabbath began at twilight, God created this ram. Thus, there was never any intention that God would allow Abraham to sacrifice Isaac. Other things God created at that time include the clothing with which God dressed Adam and Eve (thus indicating that God knew the couple would eat the fruit), the rainbow Noah saw, manna that fed the Israelites in the wilderness, and the first pair of tongs (I appreciate the logic of this last example).

As previously noted, the *Akedah* is read on Rosh Hashanah, the Jewish new year. On that day, Jews also hear the sound of the *shofar*, the ram's horn. *Genesis Rabbah* 56.10 records Abraham telling God that just as he suppressed his mercy to follow God's command, so God should, when judging the sins of Abraham's descendants, remember the *Akedah* and be filled with mercy toward them.

God Will Provide

In Genesis 16:13, Hagar names God *El-roi*, the "God who sees"; the well where she encountered the angel who assured her that her son would not only live but thrive is called *Beer-lahai-roi* ("well of the Living One who sees me" [16:14]). Abraham, assured that his son will live, calls the place of the *Akedah* "The LORD will provide" (*YHWH yireh*); the narrator adds that to "this day" (whatever the date the text was recorded), it is said, "On the mount of the LORD (*YHWH*) it shall be provided" or "he shall be seen" or "he is seen" (22:14).

The provision, or foresight, includes the angel calling to God a second time. Now God speaks directly. This morphing between the angel and God, which occurs elsewhere, such as at the burning bush (Exodus 3:2, 4; see also Judges 16 with Gideon), shows the mystery of revelation and the various ways in which God communicates with humanity. It can also show, on the narrative level, that now, instead of an angel, God returns to speaking with Abraham. Source critics suggest that these last four verses, Genesis 22:15-18, come from a different source. They may be correct, but we should not be prohibited from trying to make sense of the narrative as it stands.

God swears by the divine self, for there is nothing else by which God could swear (22:16). Now we learn that the blessings that God gave to Abraham were prompted by Abraham's obedience. We may again have different sources at play, or we may have multiple ways of understanding the relationship between humanity and divinity. The Bible gives options that work together: divine grace and human response; divine reward for human fidelity; a mystery of how the relationship begins and how it will play out.

In this retelling, because Abraham does not withhold his son, he will receive numerous offspring. More, they will be safe: they will "possess the gate of their enemies" (22:17; the idea repeats in the blessing to Rebekah in 24:60). I am not thrilled with the notion of taking over an enemy's stronghold, but I'd prefer that to conquest. The text prods me to think about what kind of blessing I would want for my children and my children's children, down the generations. Peace would be one. Health, happiness, but also that they would be kind and compassionate; that they wouldn't be stupid (variously defined). You may have other views.

One of those wishes, or blessings, is that "by your offspring shall all the nations of the earth gain blessing for themselves, because you have obeyed my voice" (22:18). Our actions can have positive or negative repercussions for people we do not know. What we do, small deeds to major moves, from medical breakthroughs and peace treaties to a kind word and or a small donation, can serve as a blessing for others. It would be lovely if we could say of our nation, people, community, or family that we were a blessing to others, and that our children were seen as bringing a blessing as well.

The Aftermath

The story ends when "Abraham returned to his young men" and they go together to Beer-sheba (22:19). Where is Isaac? The last time we saw him, he was still bound to the altar. One midrash suggests he was taken to heaven, where he studied Torah with Enoch (I am reminded of sending the last child off to college). Could be. Another is that Abraham actually killed Isaac, and God then resurrected him. Yet another is that Abraham returned to Beer-sheba while Isaac went to see his mother in Hebron, which is where she dies (23:2).

The blessings at the end of the chapter suggest that Abraham passed the test. Abraham receives a reiteration of the covenant, with the promises extending through the generations. Everything works out well.

Yes, and perhaps Abraham also tested God. In showing that he was willing to go through with the sacrifice, he forces the divine hand to reverse the command to slaughter Isaac. Thus, Abraham knows that God can be trusted.

Or, perhaps Abraham failed the test. Granted, this is not the traditional reading, and there is much in the text that speaks against it, but I still find this an intriguing possibility. One Jewish tradition, while recognizing the praise the Bible gives to Abraham, faults him nevertheless: he should have protested the test, as Hagar protested when her son Ishmael was near death, as Job protested when his children were killed and his body wracked with pain, as Abraham himself protested when God determined to destroy Sodom and Gomorrah, as the various lament psalms protest what they see as divine silence, inaction, even injustice.

Following this episode, God and Abraham do not speak again. Abraham and Isaac do not speak again. While Abraham returns "together" with his young retainers, he is no longer together with either of his sons. Genesis 23, the next chapter, begins with the death of Sarah. Has he passed or failed, or both? And after the near-death of a son at the hands of his father, what else is there to say?

The *Akedah* remains a mystery: Did Abraham pass the test by prioritizing love of God over love of his child? Did he fail the test for not protesting it? Or did Abraham put God to the test, to prove that God is the one who is merciful?

If we were asked to sacrifice not just something, but someone precious to us, how would we react? To whom do we owe our loyalty, God or our children? Our faith or our posterity? Our conscience or our theology? We are all heirs to traditions of martyrs who gave their lives and the lives of their children for their religious beliefs. Would we do the same, or would we do what we could to preserve our lives and the lives of our children?

CHAPTER 5

Jacob's Dream at Bethel

Jacob is Esau's younger twin, and the two were already at war in utero. Their mother Rebekah, in agony over their prenatal fighting, complained to God, "If it is to be this way, why do I live?" (25:22). God's response: "Two nations are in your womb, / and two peoples born of you shall be divided; / the one shall be stronger than the other; / the elder shall serve the younger" (25:23). When the children are born, the younger Jacob is grasping Esau's heel; the name "Jacob," derived from the root meaning "heel," connotes "one who takes by the heel" or "supplanter" (25:26).

True to his name, Jacob will consistently seek to replace his brother. First, when Esau returns from hunting and is famished, he asks Jacob for some of the lentil stew he is cooking: "Let me eat some of that red stuff" (25:30). The Hebrew is even less articulate: Esau asks for "red, red, that." Jacob then proposes that Esau barter his birthright for the soup. Next, with his mother's complicity, Jacob covers his arms with goat skin to mimic his brother's hairiness and tricks Isaac into giving him the blessing of the firstborn (27:1-29).

Biblical narrators rarely tell us what people are thinking. I do not know whether Jacob regretted how he treated his less astute brother or his blind father. He may have felt that he was fulfilling God's prediction to Rebekah that he would usurp his older brother's place. He may have regarded Esau as having missed priorities or as unlikely to be a proper leader. And yet, when Rebekah tells him to pretend to be Esau, he responds, "Perhaps my father will feel me [to check for hairy arms], and I shall seem to be mocking him and bring a curse on myself and not a blessing" (27:12). There is no guilt or shame here; rather, Jacob is concerned about getting caught and being cursed. His mother assures him, "Let your curse be on me, my son; only obey my word" (27:13).

Has Jacob, like Abraham, engaged in the teleological suspension of the ethical: lie to his father for the goal of gaining the covenantal blessing? Arguing that the end justifies the means makes me nervous. Is Jacob comforted by the fact that his mother has encouraged him to engage in this ruse? Is he hesitant to disobey his mother, even if her suggestion means tricking his father? I also wonder about Isaac. Does he know that Jacob is pretending to be Esau? Does he go along with the ruse to have plausible deniability when Esau asks for his own blessing? I suspect that the biblical narrators would be pleased with these questions. The stories provoke.

Esau, cheated out of his blessing, becomes enraged (I would be too) and threatens to kill Jacob (I doubt I'd go this far, but I might think of suing). We've seen this motif before: Cain, perhaps incensed that his younger brother received divine approbation, kills him. Noah's son Ham does something to him, and the result is that Noah curses Ham's son Canaan: "lowest of slaves shall he be to his brothers" (9:25). Sarah might have suspected that Ishmael, Abraham's older son, was a threat to Isaac, the younger, and demanded his banishment. The stories of Genesis offer permutations of sibling rivalry. Likely, they are recorded, in part, to encourage us to consider how families can break down and break apart and so work to prevent harm from occurring.

Rebekah arranges for Jacob to flee to "my brother Laban in Haran, and stay with him a while, until your brother's fury turns away—until your brother's anger against you turns away, and he forgets what you have done to him; then I will send and bring you back from there. Why should I lose both of you in one day?" (27:43-45). Her repetition of the notice of Esau's fury shows how concerned she is for Jacob's safety.

Rebekah is a new Eve. As the first woman handed the man the forbidden fruit and ate, she changed forever their family and their home. So Rebekah, dressing Jacob as Esau, changes forever her life with her husband and family. Rebekah assured Jacob, "on me be the curse," and so we are reminded of the curse of the land. She fears that one son will kill another, and she will lose both. The curse she invoked likely came to fruition. While the Bible does not record Rebekah's death, it also gives no indication that Rebekah saw Jacob again. Sending Jacob away becomes a sacrifice Rebekah makes.

Rebekah is also concerned about losing Esau, even though she has a prediction that he will serve his brother. I also wonder about her comment regarding Esau: she appears to expect his anger to abate. Is this because Esau blows hot and cold emotionally? Or does she know her older son to be a kind man who would not bear a grudge and who loves his younger, clever brother? Or is she dissembling to Jacob so that he would agree to leave?

Jacob flees, falls in love with his gorgeous cousin Rachel, and agrees to work for Laban for seven years in order to marry her. On the evening of the wedding, Laban substitutes the older sister, Leah, for the younger Rachel. Jacob, who supplanted his brother by tricking his blind father, is treated in kind by being tricked in the dark. Some early sources suggest that Jacob could be easily tricked because he was drunk that night (echoes here of Noah!). Whatever the explanation for Jacob's inability to realize he had been with Leah, Laban tells him the next morning, "This is not done in our country—giving the younger before the firstborn" (29:26). If we applaud Jacob's ruse, do we applaud Laban's as well?

I find myself increasingly sympathetic to the Bible's older children. God rejected Cain's sacrifice, and in the aftermath, Cain killed Abel. Had God accepted the sacrifice or done more to prevent the murder, perhaps the brothers would have lived in peace. Sarah urges Abraham to expel Ishmael and his mother, Hagar. Perhaps Ishmael was abusing Isaac; perhaps Sarah was simply jealous. Esau is tricked out of his birthright and blessing. And now Leah is placed in the bed of a man who loves her younger sister. Yet Cain holds a mark of protection, Ishmael not only becomes the father of a great nation, but he also helps Isaac bury the body of their father. Jacob and Esau will reconcile.

As for Leah and Rachel, one midrash from *Lamentations Rabbah* posits that Rachel positioned herself underneath the wedding bed. When Jacob spoke to his bride, the answers came not from Leah but from Rachel. This reading reminds us again of Jacob's tricking his father. Isaac had said to him, "The voice is Jacob's voice, but the hands are the hands of Esau" (27:22). Now the body is the body of Leah, but the voice is the voice of Rachel. While the two wives are rivals, it will be Leah's son Judah who inherits the bulk of the promise. Leah will be buried together with Jacob in the Cave of Machpelah (49:30-31); Rachel, who dies in childbirth, is buried in a separate tomb in Bethlehem (35:19).

These events of rivalry and trickery, families lost and gained, provide the context for Jacob's dream. It occurs after Jacob has tricked his father into giving him the blessing of the firstborn but before he encounters his cousin Rachel. Perhaps Rebekah told Jacob of God's prediction, "the elder shall serve the younger" (25:23). He has the blessing that should have been Esau's: "Let peoples serve you / and nations bow down to you. / Be lord over your brothers, / and may your mother's sons bow down to you. / Cursed be everyone who curses you, / and blessed be everyone who blesses you!" (27:29). He also has Isaac's second blessing:

"May God Almighty (Hebrew: *El Shaddai*) bless you and make you fruitful and numerous, that you may become a company (Hebrew: *qahal*; Greek: *ekklesia*, which becomes the term for [Christian] 'church') of peoples. May he give to you the blessing of Abraham, to you and to your offspring with you, so that you may take possession of the land where you now live as an alien, land that God gave to Abraham" (28:3-4). Jacob has multiple promises; at the same time, he is fleeing from his brother, who wants to kill him. Fulfillment of the promises is once again imperiled.

Accompanying the blessing are dangers, risks, and questions of morality and theodicy. As we travel with Jacob on his way to Paddan-Aram, fleeing his brother but with the love of his mother, in this in-between location both geographically and spiritually, Jacob has a dream that will sustain him, and his descendants, across the generations.

The Setting

Genesis 28:10 provides geographical markers: "Jacob left Beer-sheba and went toward Haran." My students tend to skip over such markers. Because the narrator took the time to mention them and because they are not needed for the plot, we do well to see whether they hold any significance. Beer-sheba first appears in Genesis 21:14; it is the wilderness where Hagar wanders after Abraham had, on Sarah's command, expelled her and her son Ishmael. Beer-sheba is a place where the desperate, the exiled, the persecuted, find God. We last were in Beer-sheba when Abraham returned from Moriah with his two young men. It is the place where God's mercy can be found. Now Jacob, like Cain, is at the mercy of God to protect him, from his brother, from bandits, from thirst and hunger and cold. Beer-sheba is a place where human and divine meet, where death turns to life, where despair turns to hope. It is a specific location; it is also everywhere that rescue can be imagined.

Beer-sheba receives its second mention in Genesis 21:31-33 when Abraham makes a covenant with the Philistines (an anachronism; the Philistines will not arrive on the shores of the land for another several centuries). This second occurrence offers an etiology: *beer* ("well"; not "beer" in the sense of Heineken or Michelob) of *sheba* (either "seven" or "oath"), hence "well of an oath." Abraham plants a tamarisk tree there and calls "on the name of the LORD, the Everlasting God" (*YHWH el-olam*). Beer-sheba is a place where people of different ethnic groups live peacefully. It is a meeting place of nations. It is a specific place; it is any place where peace is found.

In Genesis 22:19, we left Abraham and his two young men in Beer-sheba. It is the place where one goes after the divine encounter, a place to consider the past and see new possibilities for the future.

After several adventures of his own, Isaac goes to Beer-sheba. "That very night the LORD appeared to him and said, 'I am the God of your father Abraham; do not be afraid, for I am with you and will bless you and make your offspring numerous for my servant Abraham's sake'" (26:24). After the *Akedah*, I suspect Isaac appreciated the reassurance. Isaac builds an altar and calls on the divine name. This story ends with a different etiology: now Beer-sheba represents the covenant of peace that Isaac made with the Philistines, a scene repeating the covenant his father Abraham made. Beer-sheba, a place of water and wells, oaths and covenants, is also the place of memory, where covenants can be renewed. This is the location, and so the history, from which Jacob comes.

Beer-sheba prompts us to ask about the places that shaped us, and how different events—both there and in our own lives—change the meaning of the location. It also prompts me to ask about the history of the places I have lived: the origins of their names, events great and small that occurred there, and how the geography shapes those who inhabit the area.

Jacob leaves Beer-sheba and heads toward Haran. For those who are more inclined to MapQuest than vision quest, the distance from Beer-sheba to Haran is about five hundred miles. Jacob has a lot of time to think.

The name Haran applies both to a person, Abraham's brother and the father of Lot (see 11:26-27), and to the location where Terah, Abraham's father, moved the family after leaving Ur of the Chaldees. Rebekah had advised Jacob, "Flee at once to my brother Laban in Haran" (27:43). Thus, Jacob is fleeing to his mother's home, and to the one-time home of his grandfather Abraham. Jacob is leaving home, and in a sense, returning home.

Jacob may not know what to expect in Haran. Rebekah is a trickster: perhaps her brother Laban will be as well. We do not know what Rebekah told him about his uncle Laban, but so far in the Bible, sibling relations have not gone all that well. Cain killed Abel; Ham did something to his father Noah, which his brothers Shem and Japtheth seek to correct; Ishmael presents a potential rival to Isaac; and the relationship between Jacob and Esau is a tad fraught. Perhaps relations between brothers and sisters might be better. The relationship between Rebekah and Laban offers a fascinating comparison with other brother/sister stories: Dinah and her brothers (Genesis 34), Tamar and Absalom (2 Samuel 13), and Mary, Martha, and Lazarus (John 11), among others. It also prompts us to ask whether brother/sister relationships are easier to navigate than the relationships between two brothers or two sisters.

I would not date Noah, and I would not date Laban either. He first appears when his sister Rebekah informs him about Abraham's servant, who is looking for a bride for Isaac. Laban runs to meet the servant, and the narrator hints at his agenda, "As soon as he had seen the nose ring and the bracelets on his sister's arms. . . ." The first things he notices are Rebekah's new accessories (okay, I probably would have noticed the same things). The jewels are the prompt for his invitation, "Come in, O blessed of the LORD. Why do you stand outside when I have prepared the house and a place for the camels?" (24:30-31). I don't trust Laban; too late, Jacob learned the same lesson.

The Dream

Genesis 28:11 three times repeats the reference to "the place" (Hebrew *ha-maqom*): "He came to (better, he "encountered" or even "stumbled upon") a certain place (*ha-maqom*) and stayed there for the night, because the sun had set. Taking one of the stones of the place (*ha-maqom*), he put it under his head and lay down in that place (*ha-maqom*)." With all the place-naming in Genesis, this vagueness hints at a location out of time and space, everywhere and nowhere.

The term *maqom* comes to function as a circumlocution for the ineffable name of God. A (possible) biblical example occurs in the Book of Esther, a text that in its Hebrew (but not Greek) version never explicitly mentions God. In Esther 4:14, Mordechai, encouraging his niece Esther to save her people from genocide, asserts, "If you keep silent at this time, relief and deliverance will rise for the Jews from another place (*maqom*), but you and your father's family will perish. Who knows? Perhaps you have come to royal dignity for just such a time as this." God is always present, but we need to do our part.

Jacob has been on the road, and he's exhausted. The sun has set. A stone pillow is his only comfort. The text says nothing about dinner or a blanket. This is not glamping. Nor does it say anything about prayer: there is no "Now I lay me down to sleep." No "Thank you God for the blessing of allowing me to survive another day." No invocation that his journey be successful, or that his brother doesn't kill him. Cain, banished from his family for having killed his brother, worries about being killed; Jacob, escaping from a brother who seeks to kill him, expresses no worry and offers no prayer.

God calls Abraham from Haran, and God and Abraham chat often. God spoke to Isaac and blessed him. God told Rebekah about her prenatal twins. So far with Jacob, nothing. Did Jacob hear stories about God from his father and grandfather? Did he think of God as the one who blesses and promises or the one who tests? Can he take the word of his parents and grandparents, or does he need to experience this God for himself? Do we need our own revelations?

Jacob's revelation comes in a dream. The Bible is replete with dream theophanies. In 20:3, God comes to Abimelech, king of Gerar, in a dream to warn him that Sarah, whom Abraham had allowed to enter his harem (a replay of the scene with Pharaoh in Genesis 12), is a married woman. God threatens, "You are about to die because of the woman whom you have taken, for she is a married woman." Abimelech (whom I would date) protests, "Lord, will you destroy an innocent people? Did he not himself say to me, 'She is my sister'? And she herself said, 'He is my brother.' I did this in the integrity of my heart and the innocence of my hands" (20:4-5). Good for Abimelech! God agrees: "Yes, I know that you did this in the integrity of your heart; furthermore, it was I who kept you from sinning against me. Therefore I did not let you touch her" (20:6).

In 31:1-14 Jacob reports another dream to Rachel and Leah, and that dream precipitates their leaving Laban and returning to Jacob's home. Joseph's dreams alienate his brothers (37:5-11). Genesis 40 records the dreams of Pharaoh's cupbearer and baker, and Genesis 41 details Pharaoh's dream of seven fat cows and seven lean cows.

In antiquity—Mesopotamian, Greek, and Roman—dreams held value. I have friends who keep a pencil and notepad by their bedsides so that they can record their dreams. Others report recurrent nightmares: of falling, of running from a danger. Psychologists suggest that we need to dream for good mental health: dreams allow us to process fears and organize memories. Even if we do not remember our dreams, they help us in both coping and creativity.

Head on his stone pillow, Jacob dreams. He sees (Hebrew: *hinei*, here, "behold"): a "stairway" (Led Zeppelin was correct) or perhaps a ramp. The bottom is "set up on the earth" and the "top of it reaching to heaven" (the Hebrew is plural: "heavens"). The Hebrew term translated as stairway is *sullam*. To impress (or annoy) friends, you can note that the term is a *hapax legomenon*, from the Greek *hapax* ("once") and *legomenon* ("having been said"), a word that appears only once in the Bible.

On this stairway, "*hinei*, behold" [missing in the NRSVue], "The angels of God were ascending and descending" (28:12). There's a lot of "beholding" here. Look! A staircase! Look! Angels! This is no ordinary dream.

It may, however, be based on something the initial audience of this story could easily picture. The stairway could suggest the ziggurats that lie behind the story of the Tower of Babel (see Genesis 11:4 and the introduction to this book). Babylonian priests would climb to the top to commune with the gods, but in Jacob's dream, it is God who comes down once again, this time to speak to Jacob. The angels show us that the stairway is a place of communication between heaven and earth. We seek to communicate with God, and God seeks to be in communication, in relationship, with us.

One of my students, years ago, asked me why angels would need a stairway. Why not fly? The Hebrew term *malach*, as well as its Greek equivalent, *angelos*, means "messenger"; wings and halos and names such as Michael, Raphael, and Gabriel will not come until many centuries later. The Hebrew term gives us Malachi, the last prophet in the Book of the Twelve; the name is really a title meaning "my messenger." These messengers look like people (e.g., see Genesis 18 on Abraham's three visitors or Judges 13 on the angel who predicts the birth of Samson).

When I think of "heavenly messengers," I tend to think of them starting in the heavens, descending to earth, and then returning to that celestial home. Jacob has a different orientation. He sees these messengers "ascending and descending": first they go up; then they come down. Perhaps they are carrying prayers to heaven. Perhaps they reflect Jacob's own initiative, his desire to be in communication with the divine, just as much as the divine wants to be in communication with humanity.

Such communication is signaled by the repurposing of this story in John 1:51, when Jesus tells his disciples, "You will see heaven (singular here) opened and the angels of God ascending and descending upon the Son of Man." For John's Gospel, Jesus is the mediator between heaven and earth; to stretch the metaphor, he is the new staircase; for the Christian reader, he is Jacob's dream come true. Once again, the more we know about Israel's Scriptures, the better we can understand the New Testament.

Suddenly (a third *hinei*, behold!) "the Lord (*YHWH*) stood beside him." The dream of the stairway and the angels, magnificent as it is, turns out to be a prelude. Jacob is dreaming, but that does not make this theophany any less real. The Hebrew "stood beside him" could be read as "stood above it" (i.e., the pillow), but I prefer the "beside." God speaks to Jacob on the same level, not from above. This means we can talk to God, as did Abraham when he argued for the lives of the people in Sodom.

Then God speaks to Jacob. There is no condemnation of the stolen blessing. There is instead a familial connection rather than alienation; there is reassurance and blessing. God begins, "I am the LORD, the God of Abraham your father and the God of Isaac" (28:13a). The relationship is a familial one, from grandfather to father to son, and it will continue through Jacob's yet-to-be-conceived descendants. While Jacob deceived Isaac (unless Isaac knew and played along with the ruse because he thought Jacob would be the better leader), here the familial legacy is reinforced. The stories, too, will be passed from generation to generation; regardless of generational acts of infidelity, this God, attached to this family, will remain faithful.

I would have liked a reference to Sarah, the grandmother, and Rebekah, the mother, and I could imagine God celebrating blessings to them as well. Then again, this is Jacob's dream, not mine. At this point, it is up to Jacob as to whether "the God of Abraham your father and the God of Isaac" will also be "the God of Jacob."

After family comes land. God continues, "The land on which you lie I will give to you and to your offspring" (28:13b). Nowhere has just become somewhere. This is the reiteration of the promise of land made to Abraham and then to Isaac. It grounds God in both history and geography. While the borders of ancient Israel shift over time (we can think of the borders of the United States changing from the original thirteen colonies) and while the promises are not as specific as we might like (how big is this plot of land where Jacob had his dream?), God, the family, and the land remain connected, and the covenant endures. As Paul puts it in Romans 11:29, "the gifts and the calling of God are irrevocable."

Jews who attend synagogue services will hear the entire Torah read either in one year or on a triennial cycle, and thus, we hear the promise over and over. I have met Christians who have only a vague familiarity with this land promise, and many are even less familiar with its repetition. Jews and Christians both read the Book of Genesis, but we emphasize different parts and, as we saw especially in our discussion of the first three chapters, have very different reception histories. Since Christianity is not primarily ethnically based (one is "born anew" into the tradition, rather than born ethnically into it), it had no need to emphasize a particular homeland.

God continues to tell Jacob, "...your offspring shall be like the dust of the earth, and you shall spread abroad to the west and to the east and to the north and to the south" (28:14). There may be a nudge of humility encoded in the reference to "the dust of the earth." So far, God has compared Abraham and Isaac's offspring to the stars in the heavens and to the sands on the seashore (see Genesis 15:5; 22:17 [the end of the *Akedah*]; 26:4). The reference here to dust evokes the earlier uses of the term when "God formed [the earthling] from the dust of the ground" (2:7) and when God said to that earthling,

By the sweat of your face
you shall eat bread
until you return to the ground,
for out of it you were taken;
you are dust,
and to dust you shall return. (3:19)

Dust can suggest both the medium of creation and the end of life; it can also suggest the passing of one generation to the next, and with each generation, a blessing.

While the land is promised to Abraham's family, the family is not restricted to its borders (wherever those borders happen to be). The family cannot be a universal blessing if it remains only in one place (at least until the age of mass communication). We can read this blessing to Jacob as a reframing of the notice to the first humans to "fill the earth." Here, however, along with the initial concern for stewardship comes a concern that "all the families of the earth shall be blessed in you and in your offspring." The covenant community thus exists for the benefit of others. Nor does the blessing indicate that only Abraham's family should inhabit the land. Hence, the Torah consistently mandates care not only for the widow and the orphan (those less likely to have a personal safety net) but also the poor and, especially, the *ger*, the immigrant, since Abraham's family were *gerim* (immigrants) in the land of Egypt (Leviticus 19:34).

There are always blessings to go around. Jacob stole Esau's blessing from Isaac, but when Esau plaintively asks, "Have you only one blessing, father? Bless me, me also, father!" (27:38), Isaac blesses him as well. The first part of Esau's blessing is more a prediction: "By your sword you shall live, / and you shall serve your brother" (27:40a), but the ending is striking: "when you break loose, / you shall break his yoke from your neck" (27:40b). The brothers will eventually reunite as equals, both blessed with family and long life (see Genesis 25:12-18 for Esau's status). Like Hagar and Ishmael, Esau will also gain his freedom.

God's dream-message to Jacob concludes with the assurance, "Know that I am with you and will keep you wherever you go and will bring you back to this land, for I will not leave you until I have done what I have promised you" (28:15). The phrase "I will keep you" offers an echo of Cain's question, "Am I my brother's keeper?" (4:9). God is our "keeper" in the sense of guardian and protector. The promise also anticipates verses that emphasize divine guardianship. Numbers 6:24, the priestly benediction, begins "The LORD bless you and keep you." Psalm 121, a "Song of Ascents" (speaking of those ascending angels...) exults, "He who keeps Israel / will neither slumber nor sleep" (v. 4). That Jacob's name is changed to Israel makes the rest of the psalm a fascinating intertext to the patriarch's story.

This reiteration of the promise of land, of descendants, of keeping, and of blessing is to Jacob, who has fled from his home. The promise continues through the generations. The last book in the Tanakh, the Jewish Bible, is 2 Chronicles, the edict of King Cyrus, who has just conquered the Babylonian Empire and who recognizes the concerns of the Jews in exile: "Thus says King Cyrus of Persia: The Lord, the God of heaven, has given me all the kingdoms of the earth, and he has charged me to build him a house at Jerusalem, which is in Judah. Let any of those among you who are of his people—may the Lord their God be with them!—go up" (2 Chronicles 36:23). The text ends with the promise of return.

Finally, God assures Jacob, "I am with you" (Jesus echoes these words in the last verse of the Gospel of Matthew, 28:20). God has, it seems, been there all along, even if the readers, and Jacob, were unaware. More, that assurance extends to all of Jacob's descendants, and because Jacob and his descendants are to be a blessing to all, that assurance extends to every one of God's creations, all in the divine image and likeness.

Bethel

Jacob wakes. I imagine him wanting to keep the dream going but unable to hold on to it. He realizes, "Surely the Lord (*YHWH*) is in this place (*maqom*)—and I did not know it!" (28:16). God can be anywhere, in the land and in the Diaspora; in waking and sleeping, life and death. Sometimes the divine presence is more palpable; we sense it more in one place than in another, whether the kitchen over the bathroom (or vice versa) or the church over the mall (or vice versa). The problem is that we do not always realize this presence. God had been with Jacob since his conception, but Jacob did not realize it.

Jacob's "I did not know it" is a lovely sentence. It is not always easy to admit that we lack knowledge or awareness. While the word for "know" here is from the same Hebrew root that describes the tree of the "knowledge" of good and evil in Genesis 3, the context suggests a different form of awareness. Adam and Eve gain knowledge of maturity and modesty; they are no longer infants. Here, Jacob had regained the insight that little children have and adults too frequently lose: knowledge that the world is spirit-filled, wonderful beyond all imagining, a place where the divine can be encountered in stone and dust. Reading the Bible with a "willing suspension of disbelief" (the expression comes from the poet Samuel Taylor Coleridge) is a helpful exercise. We can set aside our Western Enlightenment skepticism and recapture what we find in our dreams. In this sense, Jacob has found another route back to Eden.

The NRSVue tells us that Jacob "was afraid." He proclaims, "How awesome is this place! This is none other than the house of God, and this is the gate of heaven" (28:17). The words for "afraid" and "awesome" come from the same root. I would prefer, "And he was awestruck" and said, "How awesome is this place!" The fear is not of God, or of being judged; it is not the fear that the first two humans sensed in Eden. There is no reason to see Jacob as alarmed, terrified, or scared to death, which is what "afraid" suggests to me. I do not see him acting in fear, but rather in a combination of reverence (the WOW factor) and practicality (I should *do* something). Words of comfort from a god who stands near us should not terrify us. Instead, we can act, because God is with us.

The terms "house of God" and "gate of heaven" send us back to the ziggurat and to Babylon. Supporting this connection: the name "Babylon" comes from the Akkadian for "Gate of the God(s)." Both the Tower of Babel and Jacob's staircase are thus satires on the great empire. To the empire that saw itself as the center of the world, to which all nations must come or be forced to come, the Tower of Babel is a story of failure and dispersion. To those who thought of Babylon as the heavenly gate, Jacob repositions the site from Babylon to Bethel.

The next verse, Genesis 28:18, begins, "So Jacob rose early in the morning." Not only the dream but also his reaction occurs while he is lying down. What a marvelous way to start the day: to recognize that one is in the divine presence, watched over through the night.

Jacob is not the only person in Genesis to rise early. Abraham arises in the morning to see the destroyed cities of Sodom and Gomorrah (19:27). He rises early to banish Ishmael and Hagar (21:14). He rises early to sacrifice Isaac (22:3). Such passages make me want to stay in bed until noon. But Jacob rises early to celebrate something good. Given the earlier references, my inclination is to stay in bed. Jacob provides the motive to get up.

He takes "the stone that he had put under his head and set it up for a pillar and poured oil on the top of it" (28:18b). He consecrates the most mundane of objects, a stone, and turns it into something distinct from all the other stones. Just as any place can be the site for a theophany, so any object can be shifted from the profane to the holy.

The stone becomes Jacob's marker. In the next chapter, he removes a stone from a well to help his cousin (and, in fourteen years, his bride) Rachel (29:10); in 31:45, he sets up another stone pillar to mark the covenant he makes with Laban. Genesis 35:20 states that for his beloved Rachel, "Jacob set up a pillar at her grave; it is the pillar of Rachel's tomb, which is there to this day."

Rising early and turning stones into signs of the sacred continues. According to Exodus 24:4, "Moses wrote down all the words of the Lord. He rose early in the morning, built an altar at the foot of the mountain, and set up twelve pillars, corresponding to the twelve tribes of Israel." Following in Moses's footsteps, "Joshua wrote these words in the book of the law of God, and he took a large stone and set it up there under the oak in the sanctuary of the LORD" (Joshua 24:26). Today, we think of cornerstones as markers of the sacred, or at least the important. Stones are also markers of memory. Jews do not typically put flowers on a grave. When we visit cemeteries to mourn our loved ones, we put a small stone on top of the tombstone to show that we had visited. Stones do not require a purchase; they do not require advanced planning; they do not wilt or die. Similarly, we do not typically send flowers or wreaths to families in mourning. If we visit, we bring food. We also traditionally make a donation in the memory of the deceased, so that others can be helped and so that the memory functions as a blessing.

Jacob "called that place Bethel [Hebrew: house (*bet*) of God (*El*)], but the name of the city was Luz at the first" (28:19). The unnamed place was a Luz (rhymes with booze). The place loses (couldn't resist) its original name with this replacement, but the biblical record also retains the original name. Luz means "almond" or a generic "nut," but it may also be connected to a root meaning "refuge." Names change over time; at times, they revert back to an earlier name (this often depends on who holds political power).

The name provides an etiology for Bethel, the major worship center, along with Dan, of the Northern Kingdom of Israel (Jerusalem was the center for the Southern Kingdom of Judah). Bethel and Dan will eventually be delegitimized. According to 1 Kings 13:1-2, an unidentified "man of God" came to Bethel, where King Jereboam, who led the ten Northern tribes to secede from the rule of Rehoboam, the son of Solomon, was offering incense at the altar. The man cries out, "O altar, altar, thus says the LORD: A son shall be born to the house of David, Josiah by name, and he shall sacrifice on you the priests of the high places who offer incense on you, and human bones shall be burned on you." Concerning Josiah's reforms in the late seventh century BCE,

2 Kings 23:15 reports, "the altar at Bethel, the high place erected by Jeroboam son of Nebat, who caused Israel to sin—he [Josiah] pulled down that altar along with the high place. He burned the high place, crushing it to dust." What is legitimate at one time, such as the shrine at Bethel (see, e.g., Judges 20:18; 1 Samuel 7:16), may no longer be legitimate as times, and regimes, change.

Bethel is the only place whose name means "house of God," but it is not the only "house of God." When Jerusalem becomes the central site for the Israelite sacrificial system, it also becomes the only "house of God." We can see this shift in the very frequent use of the expression *Bet(h)-elohim*, also "house of God," by later biblical authors such as Ezra and Nehemiah and the Chronicler. Any place can be a house of God, just as any stone can become sacred and any speck of dust can remind us of both death and posterity, time and eternity.

The Vow

The scene ends with Jacob making a transactional vow of the "if you do this, then I will do that" variety. Here is the "if"—what Jacob wants: "If God will be with me and will keep me in this way that I go and will give me bread to eat and clothing to wear, so that I come again to my father's house in peace…" (28:20-21a). God had already promised to be with Jacob and to protect him. Jacob specifies: bread, clothing. He does not ask to win the lottery; he does not ask to rule the world. He asks for the minimum of what he needs to live. Regarding lodging, he wants to return to his father's house. By mentioning his father, Isaac, he may be reminding God of the *Akedah* and of the fidelity of Abraham and Isaac. He says nothing about Esau, but the peaceful return can imply a reconciliation. I would have wanted him to include a blessing for his mother.

If God makes good on these items, then Jacob vows, "then the Lord (*YHWH*) shall be my God, and this stone, which I have set up for a pillar, shall be God's house, and of all that you give me I will surely give one-tenth to you" (28:21b-22). I am sympathetic to Jacob's response. Had Jacob's father and grandfather told him stories, they may have noted the sacrifices, real and interrupted, that this God has asked of them. This God wants exclusive fidelity; Jacob wants to know what's in it for him. In making this type of vow, Jacob finds himself in the company of Jephthah, in Judges 11, who vows to sacrifice to God the first who leaves his house *if* God will give him the victory. Hannah vows that, should God grant her a son, she will dedicate that son to God (1 Samuel 1). The vow once again raises the questions of the type of God we seek: one who gives, one who demands, or both? We might also consider our own relationships to God or to others: do we give, or do we demand, or both? It may be "more blessed to give than to receive" (Acts 20:35), but to give and give and receive nothing is a recipe for burnout or resentment.

The grammar of Jacob's vow may suggest that he is moving toward a more personal relationship with God. He starts by referring to God in the third person, "If God will be with me,... The Lord shall be my God," not "If *you* are with me,... *you* shall be my God." The vow shifts then to the second person, "of all that *you* give me I will surely give one-tenth to *you*." Jacob and God are now in a closer relationship: they each can give—indeed, are happy to give—the other something. Jacob wants safety, a return home, food and clothing. I doubt God is much concerned with the one-tenth; God is more concerned with being Jacob's God and so being in relationship with Jacob.

I'm also curious as to how Jacob intends to fulfill the tithe. There's an old joke about the theologian who shows God generosity with everything: "I throw the money up in the air, and God can take whatever

God wants." Because Jacob promises that the pillar shall be "Bethel," God's house, likely Jacob intends to support the temple to be constructed there.

The dream becomes a reality; the shrine Jacob started lasted for generations. His dream remains a memory and an anchor. Everyone's dreams will be distinct, but anyone can dream of that stairway whose messengers move in both directions. Anyone can turn a stone pillow into a sacred site. Any place can be, depending on the residents and the hospitality, a "house of God."

Memories of the Dream

Decades later, after Jacob and Laban have a falling out, God makes good on the promise to "keep" Jacob and fulfills Jacob's concern to return home. God advises in another dream, "Return to the land of your ancestors and to your kindred, and I will be with you" (31:3). Calling his wives, who are also Laban's daughters, Jacob begins, "The angel of God said to me in the dream, 'Jacob,' and I said, 'Here I am!'" (31:11). *Hineini*, "here I am." Jacob responds as did Abraham at the *Akedah*. After detailing the angel's instructions regarding goat breeding (I'll skip the details), he then tells Rachel and Leah that in his dream, not an angel but God told him, "I am the God of Bethel, where you anointed a pillar and made a vow to me. Now leave this land at once and return to the land of your birth" (31:13).

We find there the same shift between the angel and God that we saw at the *Akedah* and that Moses will experience at the burning bush. While source critics suggest that the texts combine two sources, one where God speaks directly and another where the angel conveys a message, we can also see such texts as preserving the divine mystery.

Jacob packs up his family and his belongings and follows the directions God gave him in the dream. Since I don't entirely trust Jacob (admire, yes; trust, not so much), I wonder whether he used the motif of the dream to convince his wives that it was time to leave. Jacob surely knows that if he stays with Laban, he will be in perpetual conflict with Laban's sons, and so, once again, he flees familial problems. Rachel and Leah, Laban's daughters, are delighted with the plan. They respond to Jacob, "Is there any portion or inheritance left to us in our father's house? Are we not regarded by him as foreigners? For he has sold us, and he has been using up the money given for us. All the property that God has taken away from our father belongs to us and to our children; now then, do whatever God has said to you" (31:14-16). What God told Jacob in the dream is exactly what Jacob, Rachel, and Leah want. The dream sounds convenient to me.

Laban, after also receiving a dream from God, realizes his son-in-law has decamped with his daughters, his grandchildren, and his flocks. He asks Jacob, "Why did you flee secretly and deceive me and not tell me? I would have sent you away with mirth and songs, with tambourine and lyre" (31:27). I've also got my doubts about Laban, whose dream seems convenient as well. After arguing about whether Jacob had "stolen" not only Laban's property but also his daughters, the two men agree to make a covenant. "So Jacob took a stone and set it up as a pillar" (31:45).

I do not doubt Jacob's original dream, nor do I doubt he experienced a divine presence at the River Jabbok (see the following discussion). But Jacob the trickster could easily have invented other dreams. Thus, he raises the inevitable question: when someone says, "I had a dream..." is the claim to be trusted?

Following this covenant, which included not only another stone marker but also a sacrifice (31:54), Jacob prepares to meet Esau. But as "Jacob went on his way... the angels of God met him" (32:1). This is the only other time aside from the dream at Bethel that the Hebrew

Scriptures mention "angels of God." No doubt here from the narrator about the supernatural nature of this encounter. "When Jacob saw them, he said, 'This is God's camp!' So he called that place Mahanaim" ("two camps"). No "behold!" here, although I doubt that, for Jacob, seeing angels is an everyday occurrence. Conveniently, the name anticipates the division he will make of his family into two parties for safety as they approach Esau (see 32:7-8).

In neither episode do the angels speak, which is odd given that they are "messengers." Their presence, therefore, requires interpretation: comfort and assurance, protection and care? There is no staircase here, so we cannot tell whether they are coming from God with divine messages of assurance or whether they are going to God with very human messages of fear. These options may be two sides of the same coin. Once the communication is established, regardless of its origin, expressions of comfort and concern overlap. God has already established the covenant. Now we hear the concern.

Nearing Canaan, Jacob fears that Esau will attack. He prays, at some length, "O God of my father Abraham. . . ." This is a good start, since in that initial dream, God self-identified as "I am the God of your father Abraham" (26:24). The next line there was "do not be afraid, for I am with you." Jacob continues, "and God of my father Isaac. . . ." Again, this is a good start, as Jacob locates himself in the family of the covenant. Here, he reminds God of the fidelity of his forefathers, and in so doing, he reminds himself of their relationship with God.

Then Jacob invokes another past event: "O Lord who said to me, 'Return to your country and to your kindred, and I will do you good . . .'" (32:9). This is an allusion to 31:3, God's statement to Jacob, "Return to the land of your ancestors and to your kindred, and I will be with you." The setting here is the run-up to Jacob's plan to take his family away from Laban.

Having established his place in the family and his previous interaction with God, he then expresses his concerns: "I am not worthy of the least of all the steadfast love and all the faithfulness that you have shown to your servant..." (32:10). Expressions of unworthiness are common in Psalms of Lament, such as Psalm 22:6, "I am a worm and not a human, / scorned by others and despised by the people." They function to contrast both the greatness of God with the (relative) weakness of human beings and to recognize the mercy and grace God shows to us. As an example of what he takes to be divine grace, he next notes, "For with only my staff I crossed this Jordan, and now I have become two companies." His concern is that his family be kept safe.

Now the plea: "Deliver me, please, from the hand of my brother, from the hand of Esau, for I am afraid of him; he may come and kill us all, the mothers with the children. Yet you have said, 'I will surely do you good and make your offspring as the sand of the sea, which cannot be counted because of their number'" (32:11-12). Reminding God of divine promises is also a component of lament Psalms. Again, Psalm 22 offers a helpful intertext. Here, the psalmist reminds God of past care, "Yet it was you who took me from the womb; / you kept me safe on my mother's breast" (Psalm 22:9). No longer is Jacob bargaining; there is no transaction here. Jacob is in danger, he is afraid, and he is entirely dependent on God.

Jacob will soon wrestle with—an angel? God? a demon? his conscience?—at the river Jabbok (32:22-32). At the end of the match, as dawn is breaking, Jacob's opponent tells him, "You shall no longer be called Jacob, but Israel [Hebrew for 'to wrestle with God'] for you have striven with God and with humans and have prevailed" (32:28). Jacob names the place "Peniel" ["face of God" or even "facing God"] because "I have seen God face to face, yet my life is preserved" (32:30). Wounded in the match, Jacob is nevertheless strengthened by another divine encounter. It seems as if every place he steps becomes a divine encounter; every place receives a new name.

There is more. Jacob is now Israel, but he remains "Jacob"; for example, we talk about "the God of Abraham, Isaac, and Jacob." When we speak of the "God of Israel," we are most often speaking about Israel, the covenant community, not Israel, the biological son of Isaac and Rebecca. All this naming, of people and places and even God, makes me wonder: If we could imagine that God would rename us, what name would we receive? If we were to find ourselves in a place where we encountered God in a particularly profound and intimate way, what would we call it? Would we return, and could we recapture that initial feeling?

When Jacob arrives, "Esau ran to meet him and embraced him and fell on his neck and kissed him, and they wept" (33:4). When Abraham died, "His sons Isaac and Ishmael buried him in the cave of Machpelah" (25:9). Now, Esau and Jacob reconcile. Later, Joseph will reconcile with his brothers. Harms are not erased, and very often what goes around comes around, but they also do not control the narrative.

A Retelling

Cain and Abel made the first altars, even if only implicitly mentioned somewhere east of Eden (4:3-4). Noah builds an altar and offers a sacrifice after safely leaving the ark (8:20). Abraham places altars throughout his travels (12:7, 8 ["with Bethel on the west"]; 13:4, 18; 22:9 [*Akedah*]). Isaac erects an altar (26:25), Jacob builds altars, and so do Moses, the Judges, and the prophet Elijah. The land is slowly being consecrated. Yet, with Josiah's reforms, the various altars will come down, with only the one in the Jerusalem Temple remaining.

I am struck by the Bible's insistence on remembering the past, on honoring the setting of Bethel, even though the shrine there becomes deconsecrated. I have been in a number of churches and synagogues that no longer function as sites of worship: They are now private homes, banks, restaurants, spaces for public art, etc. I always wonder what stories those walls could tell, of baptisms or *yizkhor* prayers, of weddings and funerals.

After Jacob has wrestled at the river and prevailed, reconciled with his brother Esau, and disputed with his sons regarding how to respond to the attack on his daughter Dinah (Genesis 34, a painful text that deserves its own commentary), God commands him, "Arise, go up to Bethel, and settle there. Make an altar there to the God who appeared to you when you fled from your brother Esau" (35:1). In 28:20-22, Jacob stated that the stone he had set for a pillar "shall be God's house." God now nudges him: go build that house.

Jacob tells his family and all in the household (including servants and, probably, enslaved people) "Put away the foreign gods that are among you, and purify yourselves, and change your clothes" (35:2). He is making good on his promise, "Then the Lord shall be my God" (28:21). He continues, "Come, let us go up to Bethel, that I may make an altar there to the God who answered me in the day of my distress and has been with me wherever I have gone" (35:3). God, who promised to be "with Jacob," remains faithful. Jacob and his family are protected on their way, when "A terror from God fell upon the cities all around them, so that no one pursued them" (35:5). We should all be so lucky when we travel. Jacob had been a fugitive from Esau and then from Laban. Like Cain, he harmed his brother, and like Cain, he is protected.

"Jacob came to Luz, that is, Bethel, which is in the land of Canaan, he and all the people who were with him, and there he built an altar and called the place El-bethel [i.e., "God of Bethel" or, redundantly "God of the house of God"], because it was there that God had revealed himself to him when he fled from his brother" (35:6-7). Jacob had renamed the site, but the old name stuck, as is often the case. The idea that a shrine or temple is "God's house" does not mean that God is constrained to one location or another. God can be anywhere; God is everywhere. Such sites rather indicate that we are together with God, in God's house, and that we are part of a community, since the house is open. Such houses are distinct from personal locations, such as a mountaintop or the seashore, or places where one can feel that divine presence in an especially palpable way. The house is (more or less) permanent, and it can be a place of hospitality, of sanctuary, for all.

When Jacob had his dream, he was alone, fleeing in fear, and he had nothing. Now he has a family and wealth. His story continues to be our story. It asks: Do we build altars or pledge ourselves to fidelity when we are at rock bottom, or do we wait until we have something for which to be thankful? Do we blame God for our failures and our distress, or do we credit God with our success and our joy?

The house of God can be found anywhere there is a stone, a piece of wood, a river, dust. Any profane place can be made sacred. When we pray—for thanksgiving, for health or for peace, to pass the exam or get the job—we can imagine that heavenly staircase, with the angels ascending and descending. I have frequently thought with Jacob, "I did not know God—a sense of the holy, a word of consolation or encouragement, a vision of beauty, a song of inspiration—was in this place." I have had serendipitous encounters where the mundane becomes suddenly charged with meaning. Close your eyes and dream. And if the dream leads you, share it and do something about it.

CHAPTER 6

Joseph, Potiphar, and Mrs. Potiphar

Joseph is a hero for overcoming injustice: he saves not only Egypt but all of Mesopotamia from famine; he models reconciliation with his brothers who sold him into slavery; he promotes his Hebrew identity despite assimilationist pressure. Granted, he started with enormous privilege: he is the older son of Jacob and Jacob's favorite wife, Rachel; he is Jacob's favorite, signaled by Jacob's gifting him with a special multicolored (or long-sleeved) coat. Like his father, he receives prescient dreams from God, and he is able to interpret the dreams of others (the technical term is "oneirocriticism"). Pharaoh, Egypt's king, elevates him to the country's second-in-command. He's also drop-dead gorgeous.

I want to like Joseph, I really do. But something about him bothers me, whether it's his plan to confiscate all of Egypt's grain for seven years and then sell it back to the people who grew it at inflated prices or the tricks he plays upon his brothers or his failure to let his father Jacob know that he is alive. My concerns about Joseph should not be unexpected. While we can take Adam and Eve as models of repentance, they do try to shirk the blame for what they did. Cain kills Abel. Noah's "most righteous" status is relative to his generation, and I'm appalled by his cursing of Canaan. Abraham should have protested the command that Isaac be sacrificed, and Sarah mistreated Hagar and Ishmael. Jacob cheated his father and his brother. On the other hand, if God can work with these people, there's hope for the rest of us.

Although I don't fully trust Joseph, I find him, as I find all these other people, to be fascinating. His story, like the others covered in these pages, is a brilliantly written novella that raises the questions we do well to consider, questions of class (slave and free), ethnicity (Hebrew and Egyptian), gender (expected roles of men and women), desire (who wants what, why, and how far does one go to get that desire), truth and justice versus lies and deception . . . even accessorizing.

The Background

Literary critics suggest that a character's first actions determine how readers assess them, and readers then determine whether our initial impressions are correct. The first time we see Joseph in action is when he, age seventeen, "was shepherding the flock with his brothers; he was a helper to the sons of Bilhah and Zilpah, his father's wives, and Joseph brought a bad report of them to their father" (37:2). He's a tattletale.

The narrator then doubles down on how spoiled Joseph is: "Now Israel [i.e., Jacob] loved Joseph more than any other of his children because he was the son of his old age, and he made him an ornamented robe" (37:3). I understand the "son of his old age" comment: Joseph is the baby, and he represents Jacob's (departing) vigor. I suspect Jacob also loved Joseph more because he was Rachel's son, and Jacob loved Rachel more than her sister, the very fertile Leah. The translation "coat of many colors" comes from the Greek; the Hebrew is unclear. The same expression in 2 Samuel 13:18-19 describes the robe worn by Tamar, sister of Absalom, daughter of David, and victim of rape by her half-brother, the crown-prince Amnon. There is much to be said about Tamar's story, and she, like Dinah (Genesis 34), deserves her own chapter. For our purposes in understanding Joseph, a comparative reading tells us that Tamar, like Joseph, was the victim of unwanted sexual attention, that rape is rape regardless of whether the perpetrator is a man or a woman, and that brothers can either harm (the brothers who seek to kill Joseph; Amnon, who rapes his half-sister) or seek to rescue (Reuben and Judah who seek to protect Joseph; Absalom, who seeks to avenge the attack on his sister).

Back to Joseph: the narrator next tells us what we already know. When the brothers realize that Jacob loves Joseph more than any of them, "they hated him and could not speak peaceably to him" (37:4). Favoritism, whether God's favoring Abel's sacrifice over Cain's or Rebekah's outsized love for Jacob, creates resentment. While the parent is at fault, it is the child who must address the consequences. Joseph's response to this favoritism included not only tattling on his brothers but also boasting to them that in his dreams, all the brothers' sheaves bowed down to his sheaf (37:7) and that "the sun, the moon, and eleven stars (i.e., father, mother, and eleven brothers) "were bowing down to me" (37:9). Despite how attractive Joseph is, I'm finding this young adult smarmy.

While the brothers hate Joseph out of jealousy, "his father kept the matter in mind" (37:11). Jacob's failure to act is reminiscent of his failure to act when his daughter Dinah is raped by Shechem, prince of the city also called Shechem. Dinah's brothers trick the Shechemites, massacre all the men, and take the women and children captive. It is immediately following this violence, which would have been known to the neighboring cities, that God tells Jacob, "Arise, go up to Bethel, and settle there. Make an altar there to the God who appeared to you when you fled from your brother Esau" (35:1). On the road, in flight, Rachel will die in childbirth (35:16-19). Jacob's failure to act also anticipates David's failure to act when the crown prince rapes Tamar. Letting major problems go unchecked allows them to fester. Not everyone will turn out to be as gracious as Ishmael and Esau. Moreover, failures to act by members of the older generation are hints that it is time for a change in leadership.

Jacob again sends Joseph to check on his brothers. When they see him, they despise him as "this dreamer" (37:19), plan to kill him, and then tell Jacob that Joseph was devoured by a wild animal. The oldest brother, Reuben, insists that blood not be shed. There will be no replay of Abel's death. Reuben plans to rescue Joseph and return him to Jacob. But we already know, from Cain, Ishmael, and Esau, that the oldest brother is not likely to be the hero.

The brothers attack Joseph, strip off his fancy robe, and throw him into a pit. Sitting down to eat, they see some Ishmaelites—descendants of Ishmael, the son of the enslaved woman Hagar. Judah, the fourth son (he has his own problems, but I'd probably date him), advises, "Let us…not lay our hands on him, for he is our brother" (37:27) and proposes instead that the brothers sell Joseph to the Ishmaelites. The text reports that they then sold him to some Midianite traders for twenty pieces of silver (a high price) and that the Midianites took Joseph to Egypt (37:28).

Roles are reversed. Sarah owned the Egyptian Hagar, but Hagar's son Ishmael, fathered by Abraham, was the potential heir. Abraham, obedient to Sarah's word and God's exhortation, expels Hagar and Ishmael, and Hagar, now free, flees with her son and finds him a wife in Egypt (21:21). Generations pass, and now Hagar's descendants purchase Joseph, Sarah's great-grandson, and sell him in Egypt. Joseph, like Ishmael, will gain his freedom; like Ishmael, he will marry in Egypt. As Hagar takes Ishmael to Egypt, so Joseph will bring his family to Egypt. And in a few generations, there will be a pharaoh who "did not know Joseph" (Exodus 1:8), and this new pharaoh will enslave Joseph's family, the Israelites.

Tragic repetition marks history: the enslaved becomes the enslaver; the victim becomes the perpetrator. The Torah instructs, "The alien (Hebrew *ger*, "immigrant," "not-native born") who resides with you shall be to you as the native-born among you; you shall love the alien (*ger*) as yourself, for you were aliens (*gerim*) in the land of Egypt" (Leviticus 19:34). While understood best as a response to the Egyptians enslaving the Hebrews and then their complicity in Pharaoh's genocidal commands at the time of the Exodus, the instruction also adverts to the Joseph story, because he was the first recorded Hebrew slave in Egypt. Joseph is subject to ethnic prejudice, false charges, false imprisonment, slavery, and death. The law is based on experience and empathy: You were there; you knew what it was like; have the heart not to do this to anyone else.

The brothers take Joseph's robe, dip it in goat's blood, and present it to Jacob. Distraught, Jacob concludes, "It is my son's robe! A wild animal has devoured him" (37:33). Jacob fooled Isaac by dressing up as his brother Esau; now, garments fool Jacob. This motif will continue when Joseph comes to Egypt. Clothes do not make the person, but they can deceive.

Jacob then tears his garments as a sign of mourning. This is the origin of the Jewish custom of tearing a garment or wearing a strip of cloth cut from a larger strip to indicate one is in mourning. Jacob's other sons and daughters (37:35; this verse is how we know Jacob had more daughters than Dinah, although she is the only one mentioned) attempt to comfort him, but Jacob will not find solace.

The chapter ends with the Midianites selling Joseph to "Potiphar, one of Pharaoh's officials, the captain of the guard" (37:36). I wonder if anyone ever said to Joseph, "Don't be such a twit." I wonder if Jacob ever told his other sons, "I love you."

Potiphar

Potiphar, the man who purchases Joseph, participates in a system of enslavement. Most people in antiquity did; some do to this day, since slavery is legal in several countries and practiced with impunity in others. Assessing him with a twenty-first-century moral code finds him lacking. No doubt assessing people in our century by the morality of the future will find us lacking as well. In reading the Bible, we cannot set aside our moral views, nor should we. At the same time, we do well to understand the views of the periods we study.

The NRSVue identifies Potiphar as "an officer of Pharaoh" (39:1). The term translated "officer" (Hebrew *saris*) can also mean "eunuch." The NRSVue has no problem translating the term "eunuch" in 2 Kings 9:32; 23:11 and elsewhere, including throughout the Book of Esther. Claims that the translation "eunuch" cannot be used in Genesis 39 since Potiphar is married are incorrect: Eunuchs could, and did, marry. The one thing eunuchs could not do was father children.

Moreover, in various places and times, eunuchs served in official capacities. The thinking was that eunuchs, who would not have their own offspring to promote, would therefore not put familial concerns over the needs of the king. Further, eunuchs could also be trusted in women-centered areas, such as harems, since they would not raise questions of paternity. Understanding Potiphar to be a eunuch provides his wife (we'll get to her in a minute) an additional motive for wanting to seduce Joseph: Joseph can father children.

Potiphar, an officer, holds power and influence; that he can buy a handsome, healthy, articulate seventeen-year-old suggests that he has money. Childless, Potiphar may think of Joseph as a potential heir. He would not be the first to consider such a move. Abraham, concerned about covenantal fulfillment, asks God, "What will you give me, for I continue childless, and the heir of my house is Eliezer of Damascus?" (15:2).

It is also possible that Potiphar bought Joseph because he found him attractive. Here is another possible echo (this is material not normally presented in Sunday schools) of an earlier story. In Genesis 12, Abraham tells Sarah to lie about their marriage and pretend to be his sister. His plan is that when the Egyptians see how beautiful she is, they will take her to Pharaoh, and then things will go well with Abraham. She complies, and so Abraham profits from Sarah's situation (we do not know whether she was happy in Pharaoh's house). Sarah is a Hebrew in an Egyptian household, where she is expected to have relations with Pharaoh. After plagues break out, Pharaoh says to Abraham, "Why did you say, 'She is my sister,' so that I took her for my wife?" (12:19). Now Joseph may be in the same position: expected to have relations with his Egyptian lord.

So far, we know nothing about how Joseph feels concerning the plot to kill him, his being sold by his brothers and bought by Ishmaelites (and/or Midianites), his being sold again and bought again. He may have found solace in his dreams: He knew that others would bow down to him. He may have understood the God of Abraham, Isaac, and Jacob to be protecting him. Or, he may have counted on his talents to protect him.

Despite being enslaved, Joseph "became a successful man" (39:2). In antiquity, enslaved people could enslave others; they could earn money; they could buy their freedom. Not only is Joseph doing well, but the narrator also repeats both that "the Lord (*YHWH*) was with Joseph" and that "His master saw that the Lord was with him and that the Lord caused all that he did to prosper in his hands" (39:2-3). The promise was that Abraham's offspring would be a blessing to others. Joseph is a splendid example of one way that promise comes to fruition.

How Potiphar knew about *YHWH* remains unexplained. It is possible that whenever Joseph succeeded in a task or promoted a good idea, he explained that he was blessed by God. Or perhaps Potiphar knew that some circumcised men were connected to the God of Abraham, Isaac, and Jacob. Perhaps Joseph had specific forms of worship or refused to participate in other forms.

And perhaps Joseph has learned to stop blowing his own shofar. Telling his family that it is God's will that they all bow to him is not helpful (even if he did dream it). Doing something helpful rather than tattling is a better way to make friends and gain respect.

Joseph "found favor in [Potiphar's] sight" so that Potiphar promoted him to head of the household (39:4). The expression "found favor" has appeared before, and it sometimes comes with a warning. Noah "found favor" (6:8), but the next three chapters depict massive destruction. Abraham finds favor with the three visiting strangers (18:3); while they convey the good news of Sarah's impending pregnancy, they are also on their way to Sodom, where things do not go well (19:19); Jacob "finds favor" with Esau (33:10), which is great, but in the next chapter Shechem seeks to find favor with Jacob and his sons, and the result will be another massacre (34:11). Favor, unless it comes from God, can be fleeting.

Meanwhile, Potiphar's purchase of Joseph is paying off: "From the time that he made him overseer in his house and over all that he had, the Lord blessed the Egyptian's house for Joseph's sake; the blessing of the Lord was on all that he had, in house and field" (39:5). The notice now explicitly recollects the covenantal promise, "I will bless those who bless you" (12:3). Potiphar, taking it easy, "had no concern for anything but the food (Hebrew *lechem*, literally 'bread') that he ate" (39:6). Here I am concerned: delegating tasks can help avoid burnout, boost trust, and open mentoring relationships. However, ditching all responsibility save deciding what to eat for dinner is both indulgent and foolish. Potiphar is supposed to be "the captain of the guard," but he is neither captaining nor guarding. That he cannot control his wife, or others under his roof, suggests a lack in Egypt's security system. Some early commentators suggested that "bread" is here a euphemism for "wife," so that Joseph has access to everything save for Mrs. Potiphar. To this point in the story, however, we have not met Mrs. Potiphar.

Mrs. Potiphar

Verse divisions do not enter the biblical text until the thirteenth century. The division in Genesis 39:6 creates a possible non sequitur. The verse reads, "So he left all that he had in Joseph's charge, and with him there he had no concern for anything but the food that he ate. Now Joseph was handsome and good-looking." The next verse introduces Mrs. Potiphar: "after a time his master's wife cast her eyes on Joseph and said, 'Lie with me'" (39:7). The versification connects Joseph's beauty with Potiphar's abdication of responsibilities (which could suggest something about Potiphar's feelings toward Joseph), but it disconnects Joseph's beauty with the wife's notice.

Here's one possible explanation for this break. Mrs. Potiphar saw something "after a time" or, better, "after these things" (39:7). As with the *Akedah* (Genesis 22), we should ask, "After what things?" Mrs. Potiphar approaches Joseph only after she has seen how everything he does works out well; she is attracted to him not only because of his beauty but also because of his talents. I suspect she did a cost-benefit analysis: she decided that he was "good for" relationships, that he was "a delight to the eyes" and that he was "desired to make one" aware of maturity (yes, I'm evoking Genesis 3:6, the woman's assessment of the tree of the knowledge of good and evil). Perhaps she concluded that sex with Joseph would be an improvement over whatever relationship she had with Potiphar. Perhaps she concluded that Joseph would make a fine candidate for fathering her child.

We can do more. "After these things" could refer to signals that Joseph is sending. One midrash (*Genesis Rabbah* 87.3) suggests that

Joseph welcomed Mrs. Potiphar's attention. The teenager, enslaved, might have thought that a relationship with the master's wife could give him an advantage. In this situation, he is comparable to Hagar, who, upon finding herself carrying Abraham's child, perceives herself to be in an elevated position in the household. Genesis 16:4 states that when she realized she was pregnant, Hagar "looked with contempt on her mistress" (the Hebrew is more eloquent: "her mistress became light in her eyes," a pun that works on both the physical level, since Hagar is pregnant and Sarah is not, and on the metaphorical level, since Hagar now has more weight in the household).

Even more, the account of Joseph and Mrs. Potiphar comes immediately after Genesis 38, a break in the Joseph story that recounts how Tamar, Judah's daughter-in-law (she deserves her own chapter), manipulates Judah into impregnating her. The biblical narrative sets us up to think that something sexual is about to happen.

As for Joseph's being "handsome and good-looking," the description evokes that of his mother Rachel, who, according to the NRSVue, was "graceful and beautiful" (29:17). The Hebrew, although for Rachel in the feminine and Joseph is the masculine, *is exactly the same.* Thus, Joseph is "graceful and beautiful." The midrash (*Genesis Rabbah* 87.3) suggests that Joseph even called attention to himself, as if he were in the marketplace "grooming his eyes, curling his hair, and lifting his heels." He is the sort of person who would appeal to both men and women. And he knows it.

Being beautiful is not always an advantage (although, admittedly, it's one I'd like to have). Abraham says to Sarah, "I know well that you are a woman beautiful in appearance" (12:11, lit: "good-looking," the same expression used for Joseph), and within three verses, Sarah finds herself in Pharaoh's household (she is not simply visiting).

Beauty, especially if one is in a vulnerable position such as being an ethnic minority without a community safety net, or being petite among physically stronger people, can pose a danger. Deuteronomy 21:11-12, concerning war captives, details provisions designed to protect "among the captives a beautiful woman whom you desire and want to marry." First Samuel 9:2 describes Saul as a "handsome young man," but his life will be tragic. David is "ruddy and had beautiful eyes and was handsome" (1 Samuel 16:12). He's the perfect politician. And yet God warned Samuel, the prophet who had anointed Saul, "Do not look on his appearance or on the height of his stature, because I have rejected him, for the LORD does not see as mortals see; they look on the outward appearance, but the LORD looks on the heart" (1 Samuel 16:7). We continue to look at outward appearances: the movie stars and athletes and "real housewives" who populate our social media are beautiful people. The Bible warns against judging books by their covers.

After these things, Mrs. Potiphar commands Joseph, "Lie with me" (39:7). She is the wife of the enslaver; she can give orders to the enslaved in the household. He's caught. To obey the master's wife means betraying the master. To refuse to obey will likely make her his enemy. On the other hand, who's going to tell? Surely not Joseph: that's one brag too far. And surely not Mrs. Potiphar, who is in no position to broadcast to her husband that she has made Joseph her toy. We can also note that Mrs. Potiphar puts Joseph in the position of Hagar, placed into Abraham's bed by Sarah, and in the position of both Sarah and Rebekah, placed in foreign harems by their husbands.

Joseph takes the moral high ground and refuses. His words echo the narrator's description of the situation under Potiphar's roof: "Look, with me here, my master (*adoni*) has no concern about anything in the house" (39:8). Potiphar is "his master" just as Mrs. Potiphar is "his master's wife." Both Joseph and Mrs. Potiphar are thus in a sense the property of Potiphar, so they could have formed a helpful alliance. Or perhaps Mrs. Potiphar sensed that her husband bought Joseph to keep her entertained (you can define the details yourselves). Is she desperate for a child? For intimacy? We know what Joseph looks like; how should we picture Mrs. Potiphar, and does our image influence how we understand her character?

He then explains that his master has given him control over everything in the house, to the extent that "He is not greater in this house than I am. . . ." We should stop here. Yes, Potiphar is greater; he has the final say on what happens or does not. Joseph may be technically correct given that Potiphar has abdicated his domestic responsibilities, but the fact remains that Potiphar is the master, not the enslaved. Joseph's ego is showing, and it's not, at least to me, attractive.

Joseph continues, "Nor has he kept back anything from me except yourself, because you are his wife" (39:8). The narrator had noted that the only thing Potiphar needs to consider is what he eats. Nothing was said about the wife. It is Joseph who sets up the restriction. We might compare him to the woman in Eden, adding to the description regarding the tree: no eating and *no touching* (3:3). Connections to Eden anticipate what follows: something about nudity, a concern for clothing, accusations of wrongdoing, punishment tempered with mercy, and new opportunities. We shall not be disappointed.

Joseph concludes his response to Mrs. Potiphar with a theological rationale: "How then could I do this great wickedness and sin against God?" (39:9). Finally, someone speaks about sinning against God. "Sin" has not been noted much to this point. It lurks in Genesis 4:7, crouching at the door and desiring Cain. It marks the cities of Sodom and Gomorrah, bound for destruction (18:20). It is part of Jacob's rhetorical strategy in escaping Laban's household (31:36). Now it is here. In all these cases, the sin is interpersonal in that it concerns what we do against others: murder (Genesis 4), lack of hospitality extending to potential rape (Genesis 19), exploitation and economic threat (Genesis 31), and, here in Genesis 39, marital betrayal. For the Bible, to hurt another, to violate another's trust, to covet what belongs to or is dedicated to another, is to sin against God.

While Potiphar saw that God was with Joseph, it is not clear that Mrs. Potiphar has such theological awareness. She continues to pursue Joseph, but "he would not consent to lie beside her or to be with her" (39:10). The scene reminds me of a workplace environment where the boss's advances force the employee to avoid being in the same elevator, the same room, or on the same floor. Now, Joseph, the tattler, cannot tattle, since he is in no position to make negative comments about his master's wife. There is no human resources office to which to complain. What does one do? What would we do if we were in Joseph's sandals?

I'm also feeling some sympathy for Mrs. Potiphar, as I did with Cain. Had she only said, "lie with me," we could attribute her interests to a desire for physical pleasure, the possibility of conception, or both. But that second phrase, "to be with her" can suggest companionship. As the "master's" wife, she is in no position to be friends with the household. Maybe she wants someone to be "a helper as her partner" (paraphrasing 2:18).

The fateful moment comes. One day, Joseph enters the house to work, and no one else is home. I doubt he was the only enslaved person in the household. There would have been cleaners, cooks, a hairdresser, a launderer, and others needed to run an estate. On this day, the only person present is the wife. I wonder whether Joseph knew she was alone. He has control over the household, which would include knowing who was where and when. Was Joseph perhaps tempted to taste what was forbidden to him?

Mrs. Potiphar grabs his garment and again commands, "Lie with me!" That he was close enough for her to grasp his garment suggests that he was not avoiding her. In the Babylonian Talmud (*Sota* 36b), one rabbi suggests that "to do his work" (39:11) is a euphemism for sexual activity; another rabbi disagreed. *Sota* 36b continues with yet another rabbi positing that Joseph was ready to succumb to Potiphar's wife, but then he had a vision of his father—a psychological cold shower—telling him to flee.

Whatever the prompt, Joseph refuses to obey her command. Good for him. He also likely realized that Mrs. Potiphar would react negatively to this rejection. So do the young actors who say no to the casting couch. So do employees and graduate students and Sunday school teachers who say no to the boss or the professor or the pastor. Integrity should be more important than the job. Nor should we want to work for, or study with, people who would take advantage of their positions. I mention this point because in discussing Joseph's "no" in classes and workshops, numerous people—both men and women—have confided in me that they were in the same situation. Some did what was expected of them, from smiling at sexually harassing comments rather than protesting, to remaining silent after the unwanted touch, to succumbing to even more difficult situations. It can help to know that the story of Joseph continually tells us that God was with Joseph, and so God was with them. Those who say no to injustice are heroes. Yet not everyone is in a position to say no. Allowing the abuse to continue to preserve the job and so support the family, remaining silent and so protecting one's family, staying in the program and one day being in a position to change it are understandable responses. For an enslaved person, whose body belongs to the master, to say no risks death. Working through the text helps people give voice to these feelings as well.

Then Joseph "left his garment in her hand and fled and ran outside" (39:12). Genesis 39:6 stated that Potiphar "left all that he had in Joseph's charge" (the Hebrew says "left…in Joseph's hand"). Now Joseph has "left" his garment "in her hand." He is naked, as were the first man and the first woman, and he knows his nudity makes him vulnerable.

Joseph's brothers took his garment, dipped it in blood, and manipulated Jacob into thinking Joseph had been killed. Mrs. Potiphar takes Joseph's garment, and she, too, uses it as a prop for false witness. Jacob used lambs' skin to fool Isaac. Likely, Laban used a veil to deceive Jacob into thinking that he was marrying his beloved Rachel rather than her older sister Leah. Garments are signs of maturity and knowledge (so Genesis 3), but they can also be our undoing.

Joseph, stripped of his trappings—of his ornamented robe, his father's favoritism, his status in Potiphar's home—needs to reconstruct his identity. Each time he is reborn, naked, perhaps to become a better person with each iteration. Joseph will change clothes again in 41:14 when Pharaoh summons him from the dungeons to interpret dreams. He comes into Pharaoh's presence only after "he had shaved himself and changed his clothes." We want our advisors to look the part; we are more comfortable when we engage with people dressed in civilian clothes rather than in a prison uniform. Then, dressed as an Egyptian, Joseph can more easily deceive his brothers when they come from Canaan in search of food.

And yet, in Genesis 38, the passage that comes between the brothers' plot to kill Joseph and his being enslaved, Tamar deceives Judah by taking off her widow's clothing and wrapping herself in a veil. She is disguised, and he thinks she is a prostitute. When she becomes pregnant, Judah accuses her of adultery. She is able to prove her innocence and Judah's paternity by producing his staff, signet, and cord. Sometimes clothing testifies to the truth. Sometimes people who do something wrong, like Judah, can admit it.

The Accusation

The wife "called out to the members ["men of" or "people of"] of her household" (39:14). People had been there all along. She and

Joseph were not alone, or if they were, they were not alone for long. Joseph could have cried out. He does not. Then again, the people in the household, under his total control, may not be likely to help. We know Potiphar really likes Joseph, as did Jacob. Therefore, we might conclude that just as Jacob's other sons resented Joseph, so, too, did the other members of Potiphar's household. They may have been jealous of Joseph, as were Joseph's brothers. Joseph may well still be a twit and a tattletale.

The wife then finds exactly the right tone first by playing the class card and aligning herself with the other members of the household controlled by Potiphar through Joseph: "See, my husband [the NRSVue correctly notes that the Hebrew says "he"—I imagine that unnamed but obvious "he" as dripping with sarcasm] has brought among us. . . ." With that "he," Mrs. Potiphar suggests that she and everyone else in the household are under "his" control; he is the master, and they are all his subordinates. Their level of resentment may well be high, and Mrs. Potiphar taps into that concern.

Mrs. Potiphar had been pursuing Joseph for quite a while, and the house was not always empty. Household retainers knew what had been going on, but like Joseph, they were in no position to tell Mrs. Potiphar to stop her advances or to tell Potiphar what his wife was doing. The household members are complicit in not speaking up on Joseph's behalf. Perhaps their resentment of his role in the household overcame their moral sense. However, being a whistleblower is not always a safe position, any more than tattling is. The story asks whether we should report such behavior as the wife displays to human resources or whether we should mind our own business.

The wife then plays the ethnic card: "He has brought among us a Hebrew to insult us" (39:14). Potiphar is an Egyptian, and while we do not know the ethnicities of either the wife or the others in the household, that "Hebrew" reference suggests that Joseph is the only Hebrew in the household.

The term "Hebrew" more generally signals an outsider status. It first shows up in 14:13 to identify how a messenger told "Abram the Hebrew" about the capture of his nephew Lot. The second use is here, and the rest of the uses in Genesis concern Egyptians speaking of the Hebrews or Joseph speaking to Egyptians, such as when he describes to Pharaoh how he "was stolen out of the land of the Hebrews" (40:15).

When people ask me where I am from, the answer I give often depends on where I am. If I am in England, I respond, "The States." If I am in Missouri, I respond, "Tennessee." In Jewish worship, we Jews do not use "Jew" or "Hebrew" to define ourselves: we self-describe as "children of Israel" or "Israel" (in the sense of the covenant community, not today's nation-state). In children's books written by and for Christians, the people in the "Old Testament" are rarely identified as Hebrews, Israelites, or Jews (with the exception of Queen Esther). They are rather "God's people" or something along those lines. Thus, Christian children miss the chance to learn that Joseph and Mary, Peter and Paul, and Jesus are all Jews. The question of how we present ourselves to others should help us think about how we present people of the Bible as well.

Mrs. Potiphar's term for "to insult" (in Hebrew *l'tzachek*) is derived from the root for "laughter" (Isaac [21:6], in Hebrew *yitzchak*). The translation "insult" is not quite apt. The term describes what Sarah saw Ishmael doing, perhaps with Isaac (21:9), and what Abimelech saw Isaac doing with his wife Rebekah (26:8). While the second example could connote "making love," the first use suggests something more untoward. Thus, Mrs. Potiphar's nuance is more along the lines of "laughing at us," "toying with us," or even, well, fill in a less savory term. Mrs. Potiphar, with splendid political acumen, sets up a double "us against them" situation in which "we" (Mrs. Potiphar and the household) are the moral victims, and "they" (Potiphar and Joseph) are the evil ones.

She continues by charging Joseph with attempted rape: "He came in to me to lie with me, and I cried out with a loud voice," and when she screamed, "he left his garment beside me" and fled (39:14-15). Household members might wonder how he "left his garment"—had he stripped it off as he was attempting to rape her? The garment could serve as a witness either for or against Mrs. Potiphar. She spins the story in as evidence of Joseph's bad intentions.

Then Mrs. Potiphar, again with splendid political acumen, set up another "us against them" scenario. She tells Potiphar that "the Hebrew servant [Hebrew: *eved*, here, "slave"] whom you have brought among us, came in to me to insult (*l'tzachek*, toy with, play with) me" (39:17). Not only does she tap into ethnic distinction, she plays into the system of enslavement: the *Hebrew* slave attacked; the Hebrew *slave* attacked. She also engages in a double deflection with the phrase "whom you have brought": it's Potiphar's fault that Joseph was in the household. She sounds like the first man, "The woman whom you gave to be with me, she gave me fruit" (3:12). She then presents the garment as evidence of Joseph's crime.

The question of when we believe people who claim harassment, or worse, and when to doubt them is not new. In light of this scene, we can look at David and Bathsheba (2 Samuel 11): Is Bathsheba the victim, or did she set up David? All such cases need to be judged on their own merits; juries do well when they assess the evidence, and they do even better when they look at the various sides of the account.

Potiphar's Response

"When his master [i.e., Joseph's master—the "his" reminds us that we have not heard from Joseph following his flight; as far as we know, he is hiding, nude, in the bushes] heard" his wife's testimony, "'This is the way your servant [again *eved*, "slave"] treated me,' he became enraged" (39:19). The "your servant" shifts the blame to Potiphar: he was the one who purchased Joseph; he was the one who gave Joseph the run of, and the running of, the household. However, at whom Potiphar was enraged remains an open question. Had Potiphar believed his wife, his next move should have been to execute Joseph or perhaps torture him to death. He does not. Instead, he places Joseph in the royal prison "where the king's prisoners were confined" (39:20). This is the designer prison: good rations, a comfortable bed, and elite companions.

I get the impression that Potiphar (a) liked Joseph, a lot, and regretted that to preserve his own honor, he needed to have Joseph removed and (b) suspected his wife of lying. He could be enraged at his wife; he could be enraged at the circumstances that work to the detriment of his household. He could be enraged at himself for not realizing his wife was eyeing his CEO. Perhaps he hoped that after a while, he could bring Joseph back, as Pharaoh will later release his cupbearer from prison and reinstate him.

A parallel case appears in the ancient Egyptian (ca. 1200 BCE) "Tale of Two Brothers" (I remember reading this in my first undergraduate class on the Bible). In this story, the wife of Anubis puts the moves on her brother-in-law Bata. Bata refuses her advances and flees. The wife makes her accusation against Bata, and Anubis believed her. However, later, Anubis learns the truth and kills his wife. Both stories pose the same question: You are the husband—what do you do? Both also show the wife to be the aggressor. How she is to be treated—killed, pardoned, ignored—is another question for discussion.

We can find parallel stories in the Bible as well, because people being "in prison" or "imprisoned" is a recurrent motif. The first example is in the Joseph story, and he provides the model for people proving their worth and finding new purpose. In 42:16-17, Joseph imprisons his brothers for three days "in order that your words may be tested, whether there is truth in you, or else, as Pharaoh lives, surely you are spies." According to Judges 16:21, the Philistines put Samson in prison (the time was long enough for his hair, the source of his strength, to grow back). Because the prophet Micaiah spoke the truth rather than stated what the king wanted to hear, King Ahab orders that he be put in prison and fed reduced rations (1 Kings 22:27). Similarly, King Zedekiah imprisons the prophet Jeremiah (Jeremiah 37). Zedekiah is then, like Samson, blinded and imprisoned by the Babylonians (Jeremiah 52:11). The psalmist prays, "Bring me out of prison, / so that I may give thanks to your name" (Psalm 142:7). From the New Testament, John the Baptizer is imprisoned and then executed by Herod Antipas (Matthew 14:1-12). The high priest imprisons Peter and John (Acts 5:17-18; see also Acts 12), Saul (later Paul) imprisons Jewish followers of Jesus in the Diaspora (Acts 8:3), Paul is himself imprisoned, several times (see Acts 16; 24–26; Romans 16:7), and Paul writes Philippians, Ephesian, Colossians, and Philemon while in prison. Finally, in his famous parable of the sheep and the goats, Jesus states, "I was imprisoned and you visited me" (Matthew 25:36).

I am *not* suggesting that everyone who is imprisoned is innocent, although some are. Often, the innocent are those who do not have the resources to fight the charges or who are charged by people less interested in seeking justice than in seeking to preserve their own positions. I *am* suggesting that people in prison should be remembered and visited; I *am* suggesting that God is with them too.

God continues to be with Joseph, so that the chief jailer finds himself in the same position as Potiphar: he "paid no heed to anything that was in Joseph's care because the Lord was with him, and whatever he did, the LORD made it prosper" (39:23). Joseph is clearly the person one would want in the household. And the blessings of the covenant continue.

And Now?

There is much more to be said about Joseph: ongoing dream interpretation, preservation of Egypt and Mesopotamia during a severe famine, testing, then reconciliation, then relocating his family to Egypt, his Egyptian wife and their two children, and so on. Here, at the end of Genesis 39, we leave Joseph in prison with questions: about pride and humility, the turning from obnoxious teenager to (less obnoxious) leader; the power of lies and evidence that can be interpreted in more than one way, assimilation and maintaining ethnic and religious identity; physical appearance and morality, about how we assess the cultural expectations regarding men and women (gender roles), the guilt of people imprisoned on charges brought by others, and much more.

In particular, Joseph's story reminds us of sexual trafficking, of how sexual harassment and worse go unreported by people who are not in positions of power; of how evidence can be manipulated in the courtroom, of how foreigners (immigrants, migrants) are often socially vulnerable, and of how untrustworthy people can be: brothers, employers, a friend made in prison, and of how the good works of one group in one generation can easily be forgotten in the next.

I do not want to end this chapter on a low note. The story of Joseph also tells us that one person can represent an entire people. I am the "first Jew" a number of my students have met over the years; I remember the first time I met a Methodist and a Presbyterian. If we make a good first impression, we may go a long way toward thwarting prejudice. And if we make a bad first impression, we threaten to damage the reputation of an entire group.

Next, Joseph is in prison, but he's doing well. We know he will be released when the chief cupbearer, whose dream he interpreted correctly, remembers—after a few years!—that Joseph might interpret Pharaoh's dreams about the fat and thin cows. We know that he will rise to power in Egypt, as he did in prison and, before that, in Potiphar's house. He will save all of Egypt and peoples in neighboring regions, including in Canaan, from famine. And he will resettle his entire (reconciled) family in the "the land of Goshen" (47:6; not, as I first heard it, "the 'Lantic Ocean" [I'm from Massachusetts; it was an easy mistake]).

The Book of Wisdom, also known as the Wisdom of Solomon, from the Deuterocanonical texts (the Old Testament Apocrypha) explains (10:13-14) that it was Wisdom (Greek: *Sophia*) who delivered Joseph from sin, descended with him into the dungeon, proved his accusers lying, and gave him everlasting honor. We can understand Joseph as brought down to the pit, down to Egypt, down to the dungeon, as learning about powerlessness, humiliation, and degradation so that he can be in a better position to lead.

He develops empathy, a good start. Genesis 42:24 reports that Joseph "turned away from [his brothers] and wept." He feels the connection in his gut (KJV "bowels"): he "was overcome with affection for his brother [Benjamin], and he was about to weep. So he went into a private room and wept there" (43:30). Then, he assuages their guilt: "Do not be distressed or angry with yourselves because you sold me here, for God sent me before you to preserve life" (45:5). He repeats, "even though you intended to do harm to me, God intended it for good, in order to preserve a numerous people, as he is doing today. So have no fear; I myself will provide for you and your little ones." The narrator adds, "In this way he reassured them, speaking kindly to them" (50:20-21). We have a revision of Genesis 4 (Cain and Abel), where Joseph proves to be a "keeper" of his brothers.

On the other hand, I don't want to downplay the harm the brothers did: the "it all turns out okay in the end" approach or the even worse "it's all for the best" cannot resolve for me the original hurt. Joseph names his firstborn son Manasseh [from the Hebrew for "causing to forget"], and 41:51 explains the name, "'For,' he said, 'God has made me forget all my hardship and all my father's house.'" Joseph is more generous than I. Not all people who have gone through traumatic experiences (and Joseph has been through a number) would have his resilience, and he cannot be the standard against which we measure ourselves. Nor could I "forgive and forget"—to forgive requires remembering what had to be forgiven. The name proves ironic: every time Joseph sees his firstborn, he cannot help but be reminded of the reason for the name.

Jacob, the grandfather, will bless both of Joseph's sons, but he crosses his hands so that the younger, Ephraim, receives the primary blessing. The child named after matters to be forgotten is, in effect, forgotten again regarding the birthright. The damage of generational hurt continues.

Nor am I convinced that the brothers have become more honest. When Jacob dies, the brothers worry that Joseph will now exact his revenge. They tell him, "Your father gave this instruction before he died, 'Say to Joseph: I beg you, forgive the crime of your brothers and the wrong they did in harming you.' Now therefore please forgive the crime of the servants of the God of your father" (50:16-17). The text nowhere recounts this wish. The Bible sometimes depicts invented comments: Ruth tells Naomi that Boaz sent grain to her (Ruth 3:17), and much later, Martha will tell her sister Mary that Jesus had asked for her (John 11:28)—both comments are inventions designed for the good of the recipient. Commenting on the brothers' statement, the Babylonian

Talmud (*Yevamot* 65b) reports, "It is permitted for a person to depart from the truth in a matter that will bring peace." The so-called white lie is another topic worth discussing.

Another massaging of an original event occurs in Genesis 40:15. Joseph tells Pharaoh's cupbearer that he was "stolen out of the land of the Hebrews." Joseph was not "stolen" or, better, "kidnapped": he was "sold" by his brothers (see Genesis 45:4). History, and life, are often more complicated than simple binaries of good and evil.

Every generation needs to be vigilant, and no one can afford to forget the past. People trafficked, or falsely accused, or betrayed can look to Joseph and have hope. Perhaps they will reconcile with those who hurt them, as do Ishmael and Isaac, Jacob and Esau, Joseph and his brothers. Our stories may carry the same plotlines of talent, betrayal, fidelity, and surprise, but it is up to us to write the ending.

EPILOGUE

New Beginnings

Coming to the end of this volume is, for me, frustrating. For each chapter, there is so much more to discuss. I wanted to talk about Dinah (Genesis 34) and Tamar (Genesis 38), about Sodom and Gomorrah (Genesis 19), and about Pharaoh's dreams (Genesis 42). Here are a few parting thoughts about each of our subjects. Ideally, you have more.

With Genesis 1, we might begin with a consideration of what it means to be blessed. On the fifth day, God creates "every living creature that moves," sees that all of creation is good, and "God blessed them, saying, 'Be fruitful and multiply'" (1:21-22). Then God similarly blesses human beings (1:28) and adds care of the earth and all that is in it. I take this care as part of a blessing, as I take the care I give to my children, and my students, as a gift to me, a blessing. To be entrusted with responsibility can be a blessing rather than a bother. We may well depend on God, but God depends on us as well to fulfill that blessing. And the world depends on us. With this start, we can look at other "blessings" in Genesis, especially the covenantal blessing, "I will bless you…I will bless those who bless you…and in you all the families of the earth shall be blessed" (12:2-3).

That first creation story continues into Genesis 2, where God blesses the seventh day (2:3). Since Genesis 3 tells us that work is not always easy, the Sabbath provides the ease. We could explore the teachings concerning the Sabbath (my next book will be on Jesus and Jewish holidays, including the Sabbath), or, more generally, how to sacralize time.

Regarding Genesis 3 and its reception over time, we might consider how we regard humanity: Are we totally depraved or wondrously made, a little lower than the angels? Can we work to undo the status quo: the double-shift many women still face of lower income and more child-care, the difficulties of labor, the enmity between humans and animals? More, how do we address the idea of a "curse": Is it the opposite of a blessing? Can it be undone? Is it of our own making rather than the way the world must work?

The story of Cain and Abel raises the ultimate moral issues. The notion that to kill one person is tantamount to killing one-fourth of the world's population leads to the conclusion that every life is of value. Every life. That "bloods" cry out continues to the point, since to kill a person is to prevent the next generation either from existing or from knowing the people who had died. Of greatest interest to me is Cain, given my work at Riverbend Maximum Security Institute in Tennessee. My insider students insist that, heaven forbid, we are known only by the worst thing we have ever done. Genesis 4 asks what the appropriate response is to murder, how the one who committed the murder, if not executed, can find ways of making life meaningful, and whether we might consider the views of the families of both victim and perpetrator.

The story of Noah and the ark bothered me when I was a child: I worried about puppies drowning, and I also did not understand how fish could drown. As a parent, I worried about how to tell this story to my children, and the cute books with the giraffes peeking out windows did not resolve the problems. I take it as a good thing that my own children raised questions about morality and ecology. How should this and other stories be taught to children? Is it appropriate to encourage children to question everything, even God, or is that a step too far?

For the *Akedah*, I want to think more about Isaac, the most under-developed of the three patriarchs; the stories of Abraham and Jacob, as well as Joseph, are more robust. We can view Isaac as an adult or a child, as knowing what is about to happen and as fully trusting in his father and his God. Or we can read him as a victim. I also wonder how he would tell his own story.

Jacob dreams of the stairway to heaven, and he also has the night-time experience of wrestling at the Jabbok River. Dreams and visions can change us. They can make us more aware of our environment, they can help us work through our problems, and they can show us a world different from the one we know during waking hours. They can tell us of a God with open streams, or steps, of communication, and they can tell us of a God who holds us accountable for what we do. In thinking of God, envisioning God, what picture do we hold: Parent or Judge, one who blesses or one who punishes? How do we make theology more of a dream and less of a nightmare?

Joseph is a survivor (he'd be great with a bunch of contestants on a desert island). He avoids Mrs. Potiphar's entreaties, he saves Egypt, he reconciles with his brothers, and he rescues his family. He is also almost murdered by his brothers, sold into slavery, sexually harassed, falsely accused of rape, and sent to prison on an unjust charge. He models not victimhood but resilience. Is he a good model or an unrealistic one? Or might it be that he also victimizes others: his brothers, his father, the Egyptians? Should he have our sympathy, our criticism, or both?

One way of assessing these characters is to cast them: Who would play Adam and Eve or Joseph? Another is to read the words the text assigns to them aloud, and see how they sound—compassionate or confused, snarky or curious, intelligent or afraid? A third is to follow them through Jewish and Christian (and sometimes Muslim) history to see how they have been understood over time by religious thinkers. A fourth is to look at their representations in art and music. And a fifth is to put them in conversation with other biblical scenes. The possibilities, like the takeaways we get from their stories, are endless. Enjoy.

www.ingramcontent.com/pod-product-compliance
Lightning Source LLC
LaVergne TN
LVHW032345080926
847665LV00043B/1888